Bon Appétit®
Summer
COOKBOOK

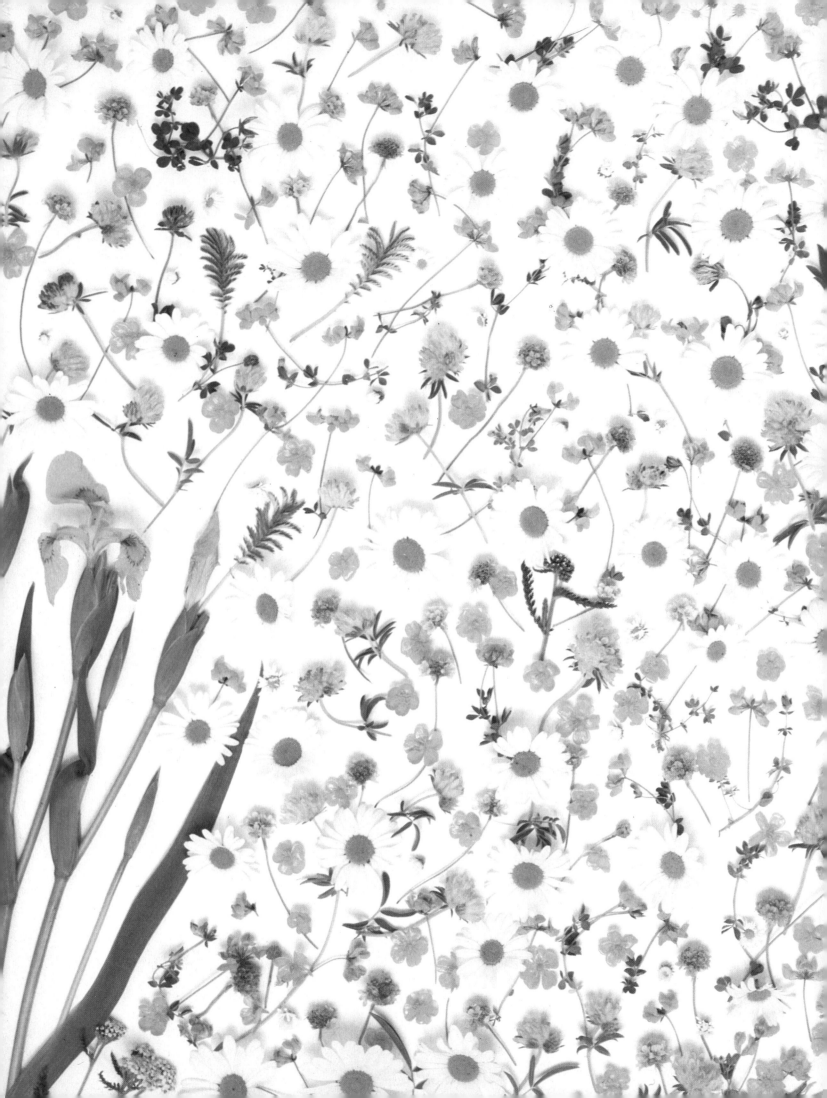

Bon Appétit®
Summer
COOKBOOK

Arabella Boxer and Tessa Traeger

The Knapp Press, Publishers, Los Angeles

Bon Appétit ® is a registered trademark of Bon Appétit
Publishing Corp used with permission

Editor	*Fiona Grafton*
Art Editor	*Val Hobson*
Assistant Editor	*Jane Garton*
Consultant Editor	*Helen Scott-Harman*
Editorial Assistants	*Atalanta Grant-Suttie*
	Amanda Lynch
Assistant Art Editor	*Ingrid Mason*
Art Assistant	*Flick Ekins*
Executive Editor	*Alexandra Towle*

Food and Wine Consulting Editor for The Knapp Press,
Gene Benton, in association with the Editors of Bon Appétit

Bon Appétit Summer and Winter Cookbook was edited and
designed by Mitchell Beazley Publishers Limited, Mill House,
87-89 Shaftesbury Avenue, London W1V 7AD

First published in the USA by The Knapp Press
5900 Wilshire Boulevard, Los Angeles, California 90036

Distributed by The Viking Press, 625 Madison Avenue, New York,
New York, 10022   Distributed simultaneously in Canada by
Penguin Books Canada Limited

Library of Congress Cataloging in Publication Data

Boxer, Arabella, Lady.
Bon appétit winter cookbook.

Issued with the author's Bon appétit summer cookbook.
Los Angeles (1980)   Inverted text.
Includes indexes.
1. Cookery. I. Traeger, Tessa. II. Title.
III. Title: Winter cookbook.
TX651.B64   641.5'91   79-21133
ISBN 0-89535-036-X

Printed and bound in Great Britain

The publishers and authors would like to thank Jan Baldwin,
Tessa Traeger's assistant, and Oula Jones who compiled the indexes.

Contents

How to use this book . . . . .

The Summer and Winter Cookbook is presented as two books
bound together under one cover. Each book is divided into two sections.
The illustrated text on seasonal cookery themes is cross-referenced to the recipe section.
The index for the Summer Cookbook begins on page 127.

Introduction

The foods that appeal most in summertime are so varied as almost to defy classification. In short, it is easier to define the foods that do not appeal: the heavy dishes, with a high starch content, or those rich in fat, which we need in winter to keep us warm. Almost all my favorite foods are summer foods. I have a strong inclination, almost a passion, for light, fresh-tasting foods: leafy vegetables, dishes in aspic, broiled meats, poached fish and salads of all sorts.

Another appealing aspect of summer eating is the opportunity of using fresh herbs. Although loath to offend the devotees of dried herbs, I must honestly admit I can find little to recommend them. Fresh green herbs, on the other hand, have just about everything in their favor. They are like the distilled essence of fresh food; full of health-giving properties, they add to our capacity to digest food, as well as giving it a delicate taste and visual appeal. They also have the advantage of distinguishing clearly the essential difference between freshly prepared and packaged food, for their is no way that their freshness of flavor can be either preserved or duplicated in any fashion.

Many of our favorite dishes change their character in summer; new potatoes, for instance, are a quite different vegetable from the floury old ones of the winter months. While these are also good, indeed better for some purposes, they cannot rival the first new potatoes, fresh from the garden, with their summery taste. Summer spinach, with its soft, almost silky texture, is another good example of a food that reaches its peak at this time of year. Crisp fresh lettuces, even the soft-leaved and tender varieties, are totally dissimilar to their winter cousins, the limp products of greenhouses and artificial heat. Young spring chickens have a character all their own, though they may lack some of the flavor of the older birds. A spring lamb, especially one that has fed on the salt marshes of Kent, Wales or France, makes one of the best dishes of all time, particularly when served with mint sauce and a fruit jelly—crabapple, red currant or quince. Salmon trout is another of our summer delights in Britain, although its cousin, the salmon, does not appear until late winter or very early spring.

In very hot weather—late summer for example—we hardly feel the need for solid food, but this can be misleading. It becomes dangerously easy to neglect our diet in muggy weather, when appetites wane and the urge to cook disappears almost altogether. Yet liquid food can be nourishing as well as appetizing, and

there are many delicious drinks, often speedily made in a food processor or blender, which are also full of vitamins. Fresh herbs combined with buttermilk; vegetable juices alone or mixed with yogurt; fruit juices; consommés of beef and chicken drunk chilled; thin purees of cooked vegetables enriched with a little cream—all these can give us nourishment with little weight. I am not often an advocate of canned foods, but in hot weather they do prove their worth. Canned clam juice can be used to make an excellent cold soup, and for those without a juice extractor, canned vegetable juice and tomato juice are worth their weight in gold. Canned tomatoes can be useful for making quick sauces for spaghetti—even uncooked, for spaghetti is often served cold in Italy, well moistened with olive oil and with a fresh spicy sauce.

Ice creams and sorbets make a perfect close for a summer meal, just as chilled soups make a good beginning. The homemade ice creams of childhood memories taste better than even the best commercial varieties. The latter have become so complex in their diversity of flavors as to make one long for simple tastes: a single acid fruit, like raspberies, makes the best ice cream, in my opinion, since they can withstand bland additions of cream and egg yolks without losing any of their pungency. Sorbets, on the other hand, seem more suited to mixtures of fruit; many of the tropical fruits make delicious water ices when combined with orange and lime juice. Citrus fruits do not combine well with cream: lime, lemon, orange and grapefruit—and pineapple as well—are all better in tart sorbets.

One of the delights of summer is eating fresh fruit quite simply, whether berries, currants, or cherries, or the fruits like apricots, peaches, plums and nectarines. This is how they have been served for hundreds of years in English country houses: as a separate course, following the cheese, which itself followed the dessert. Straight from the garden, which was usually well supplied with greenhouses to compensate for the vagaries of the English summer, the fruit course had its own special china, and even its own knives and forks, often in silver gilt to avoid the unpleasant effect of acidity on steel, accompanied by a silver sugar shaker and a small pitcher of cream. As young children in our home in Scotland, for our birthdays the head gardener would contrive to produce the first peach, raspberry, or nectarine of the year, for each of us in turn. In this way I learned to appreciate the joys of eating fruit early, but in season.

The indispensable egg

The egg has always played an important role in our culinary history, and today we recognize it as one of the most complete and economical of foods

All eggs are edible and have probably all been eaten at some time or other. Swans' eggs were once used for wedding cakes, while plovers' and quails' eggs have been considered a delicacy in England for hundreds of years.

Most wild birds' eggs are now protected by law, on both sides of the Atlantic. In England, some gulls' eggs are an exception to this rule, and surprisingly enough, plovers' eggs also may be gathered, but only up to April 14, for the plover or lapwing is one of the few birds that is increasing in numbers. Pheasants' eggs are said to be extremely good to eat but these birds are too valuable for the eggs to be eaten; as indeed is often the case with eggs of ducks and geese.

Quails' eggs can be purchased in jars, but the fresh eggs have more flavor and are more decorative. In England they are sold already cooked, and are best served as they are, in their shells, with thinly sliced brown bread and butter, celery salt and cayenne pepper.

Doves' eggs were once much used; the dovecote was not just a decorative addition to the great country houses but had a sound practical value. With all the facilities of modern life, one tends to forget the exigencies in previous times of feeding large families through the winter months. With a dovecote a supply of fresh eggs was assured, as well as the occasional bird. Dovecotes were never artificially set up; the dovecote was simply built and left empty, whereupon flocks of wild doves would arrive to fill it. Nowadays doves' eggs are protected, with the exception of the collared dove in Scotland.

The egg of the owl, like that of the dove, is almost completely round. The egg of the guillemot (a narrow-billed auk) is long and pointed, like an avocado pear. This is a form of protection, for the guillemot lays its eggs on precipitous ledges on the sides of cliffs, and if caught by the wind the egg does not roll but swings around on its axis to face into the wind.

Although early English cookbooks, from the fourteenth century onwards, contain many recipes for cooking eggs—in pastry, with vegetables, as omelettes, fritters and custards—they are rarely mentioned in accounts of meals.

I could find only three mentions of actual egg dishes as part of a meal, which puzzles me somewhat. They were certainly used in large numbers; until the seventeenth century, for example, hard-boiled eggs formed the basis of most stuffings, in the way that bread crumbs do today. Perhaps egg dishes did not figure in the sort of grand meals that were considered worthy of recording. The earliest mention I was able to find was in an account of an elaborate dinner, of 68 dishes, given in 1730; included were roast pheasant dressed with its eggs and another dish called Portugal eggs. In his *Diary of a Country Parson* some thirty years later, Parson Woodforde records a simple dinner consisting of roast mutton, veal cutlets and a selection of cold meats and eggs boiled in their shells; this was followed by a plum pudding.

In the nineteenth century the egg made its first appearance at the breakfast table. Until then a heavy meal of meat dishes with cheese and beer had been the custom among country folk, while a few more sophisticated people had taken to a light breakfast of rolls with hot chocolate. At that point the traditional English breakfast as we know it established itself: a meal consisting of porridge, eggs and bacon, or fish, followed by toast and marmalade, with coffee or tea.

In this century, England's consumption of eggs doubled just before World War I; then it doubled again before World War II. Both times, the restrictions inevitable in wartime interrupted what might otherwise have been a steady growth. Then for the first time in hundreds of years the English started to eat less; the heavy meals of the eighteenth and nineteenth centuries gave way at last to a totally new approach to food, encouraged by the emergence of smaller households and fewer children and servants. In this era of lighter meals the egg gained a new importance. Certainly by the 1920s and 1930s, an egg dish was considered acceptable as a first course for a simple luncheon or dinner. Nowadays egg dishes have become almost a way of life. As was recorded in a recent biography, all Noël Coward wanted to eat in the evening was a "little eggy something on a tray."

1 Guillemot	
2 Dove	
3 Quail	
4 Herring gull	
5 Black-headed gull	
6 Duck	
7 Ostrich	
8 Moorhen	
9 Guinea fowl	
10 Pullet	
11 Chicken	
12 Plover	

Hot-weather soups

Small china bowls of attractively garnished creamy purees, golden consommés or blends of raw vegetables, served hot or icy cold, make an appetizing start to a summer meal

1 Cold cucumber soup
2 Beet and fennel soup
3 Carrot and tomato soup
4 Gazpacho
5 Cold watercress soup
6 Crème Sénégale

Summer soups are as different from winter soups as summer frocks are from winter dresses. For a start, they are less substantial, and never form the main part of a meal, as a minestrone might in wintertime. Their purpose is quite different, and they are intended more as a prelude to a meal than as part of the meal itself. In really hot weather they may be almost more like a cocktail, or a sort of liquid salad, than solid food. In Spain, for instance, gazpacho originated as the food of the poorest peasants in Andalusia, a sort of simple salad eked out with water and eaten with bread for the midday meal. From there it traveled to the tables of smart restaurants in Madrid, London and New York, where it is popular for its very lack of nourishment, its refreshing quality that helps to revive a flagging appetite. Iced consommés are also delicious in hot weather: cold borsch, madrilène, or simply a well-made beef tea or chicken broth. When preferred, any of these may be served jellied, which makes them even more appetizing, especially when served with fresh lemons. The jelly should not be too firm, nor yet solid; it should be broken up and piled in small cups.

Only slightly more filling are the light vegetable purees; a cream of green peas is one of the best known, but more unusual is one of lima beans. Thin purees of watercress, cucumber or spinach are also good; in varying shades of green, these look pretty with a blob of lightly whipped cream floating on the top, or partly stirred in. Another good puree can be made with sweet corn, or an unusual one with zucchini. A puree of potatoes can be enriched with cream and flavored with one of the most delicate summer herbs: chervil, dill or burnet. All these soups can be served hot or cold as desired; when cold, I like to puree them to a smooth texture, and add a garnish at the last minute. A green pea soup could have a few small peas floating in it, while some tiny beans can decorate the lima bean soup. A few kernels of corn look pretty in the corn soup; the watercress soups needs only a little sprig of its own leaves. The zucchini soup is best garnished with a little sour cream, or some chopped herbs. When these soups are served hot, I like them to be slightly coarser, and leave them ungarnished.

One of the most popular of hot-weather soups is vichyssoise, with its obligatory garnish of chopped chives. Cold soups are popular in America, where vichyssoise made its reputation. One which I like even more, but never see outside the United States, is crème Sénégale. This I ate for the first time at the Knickerbocker Club in New York, and have since made it often myself. A chilled cream of chicken soup, lightly flavored with curry powder, it is a most appealing color and more than delicious.

Some refreshing and unusual soups can be made by using a combination of cooked and raw ingredients. I have devised a soup of cooked and pureed cucumbers with minced raw tomatoes stirred in at the last moment; in this way one combines the digestive qualities of the cooked vegetable with the sharp acidity of the raw one. The same technique can be used with just one vegetable; a cream of cauliflower can be enhanced by the addition of some raw chopped flowerets scattered in at the last moment.

Some soups that we connect more often with wintertime can be adapted to make interesting summer soups. A lentil soup made with buttermilk, for instance, makes a most delicious and unusual cold soup, more sustaining than most. I often use buttermilk for adding to cold soups, for it gives a smoothness and tart flavor, increased with lemon juice when desired, without the bland richness of cream. It is not suitable for hot soups since it separates as the temperature nears boiling point; to achieve a similar effect in a hot soup it is best to use a mixture of sour cream, milk and lemon juice.

A light fish soup can be excellent in hot weather, particularly when made with shrimps or other shellfish. A version of crème Sénégale, substituting shellfish for chicken, is one of the most appetizing. Saffron can be used instead of the curry powder as flavoring.

Just as the soups themselves differ from their winter versions, so should the methods of serving vary. Whether hot, cold or jellied, all summer soups are best served in small cups or bowls, preferably of thin china. Only a small amount per person is required, and since a garnish is often an intrinsic part of the soup, they are not suited to serving in a tureen. Whether of small vegetables, leaves, herbs, or simply cream, a garnish always looks better contained within a cup rather than floating about in a large soup plate.

Freshwater fish

Their excellence too often underrated, fresh fish from rivers and lakes, are delicious hot or cold with the simplest of accompaniments, and so easy to cook

Fishing may be the favorite sport of the English, surpassing even cricket. Yet despite this, freshwater fish are sadly neglected by English cooks. (In one classic English cookbook, 35 pages are devoted to recipes for sea fish and six to the freshwater sorts.) Apart from salmon and trout, river fish are rarely found on the table in either private houses or restaurants; probably the only people who ever eat our rivers' pike, shad, perch or grayling are the anglers themselves. Yet in France there are many classic dishes based on river and lake fish, including *quenelles de brochet*, *matelote* of mixed river fish, *anguilles au vert*, and many dishes of *écrevisses*, the freshwater crayfish.

While sea fish vary widely from ocean to ocean and many Mediterranean fish simply have no equivalent in Great Britain, freshwater fish seem to vary little, except possibly in flavor. The rivers of all European countries and even Russia are filled with salmon, trout, pike, perch, shad, grayling and crayfish.

Today the trout is probably the most important river fish apart from salmon, which has now joined the ranks of luxury foods, thus acquiring an unjustifiably elevated reputation, in my opinion. In days gone by, Scottish laborers used to stipulate in their contracts that they were not to be fed salmon more than a specified number of days each week. England has never been a great fish-eating country compared to Scotland, which despite the excellence of its beef has always consumed vast quantities of fish.

There are two sorts of trout native to England, salmon trout and brown trout; and a third sort, called rainbow trout, has been introduced from North America.

Salmon trout approaches salmon in price, but I consider it superior in flavor. It is a pretty fish, weighing from 1½ to 6 pounds, with delicate light pink flesh; it is not as strongly colored or as rich as the salmon. It divides its life, as the salmon does, between river and sea, and is usually caught by net in the estuaries. After being poached in plain salted water, it can be served either hot or cold, but not chilled. Served

hot with a mousseline or hollandaise sauce it is exquisite; when cold, a green mayonnaise is a good accompaniment.

The brown trout, very similar to both the European trout and American brook trout, can be found in fast-flowing streams and rivers and in deep lakes. It is one of the best fish for smoking. It has delicate flesh and very tasty skin. It can be broiled, fried or poached; baked in the oven; or filleted and fried in oatmeal as in Scotland.

The rainbow trout, introduced in Britain about 80 years ago, is now widely raised on fish farms. Although fish farming has been a highly developed industry in Denmark, Italy, Germany and Japan for many years, it has only recently been introduced in the United Kingdom.

Pike are rarely seen in shops, yet they are ideal for pounding into quenelles, mousses and molds. They are also good poached whole in a court bouillon and served with a wine-flavored sauce, or a *beurre blanc*. Shad is an excellent fish, much loved in America. Grayling, another fish not to be found in shops, is rather like a cross between a grey mullet and a trout.

In terms of food value, fish is probably better value for money than almost any other food. Trout, in particular, is rich in protein, calcium and iron. Yet half the fish eaten in Great Britain is bought at fish-and-chips shops, which is a sad reflection on our food-consuming habits.

In Celtic times, eating fish was forbidden since the rivers were thought to be sacred. With the coming of the Romans this changed, and as Christianity spread, fish-eating days were introduced and later enforced by law. Devout church-goers did not eat meat at all during Lent, or on any Friday or fast day throughout the year. In inland areas this meant that large supplies of freshwater fish were essential, especially for the large households of the time. In many ways, the well-stocked fishponds of the monasteries were like the forerunners of our modern fish farms. As early as AD 1100 the monks had succeeded in reproducing the conditions necessary for encouraging the fish to spawn successfully.

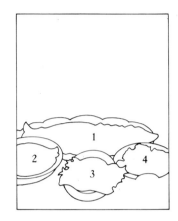

1 Poached salmon trout
2 Broiled trout
3 Cold trout en gelée
4 Trout in oatmeal

Fish from the sea

Take a fresh look at fish—their delicate flavor and texture gives endless variety to many of our best-loved dishes, and there is such a fascinating range to choose from

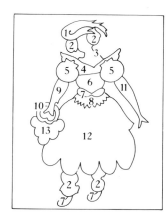

1 Lobster
2 Oysters
3 Whitebait
4 Whiting
5 Scallops
6 Sardines
7 Mussels
8 Sprats
9 Trout
10 Eel
11 Mackerel
12 Smoked haddock
13 Clams

These days most people seem content to restrict their fish buying to the frozen food compartments of the nearest supermarket. I don't know why we are so lazy about preparing fresh fish, because the actual cooking time is short—even the largest fish can be cooked in half an hour—and the results are so delicious.

Fried fish is one of my favorite dishes; I prefer it coated in bread crumbs rather than the batter usual with fish-and-chips. Batter necessitates frying in deep oil which I avoid whenever possible. I have experimented with frying all sorts of fish in shallow fat and find it perfectly satisfactory, although the results do not always look quite so professional.

When I first started cooking, I used to make endless dishes of fillets of fish baked in the oven with various garnishes; now I much prefer fish cooked absolutely plainly, either broiled, fried or poached, and served with a separate sauce. I think almost all white fish is good fried: little strips of Dover sole are exquisite, but even quite dull fish is good when carefully fried. I make a huge platter of several different sorts and shapes of fried fish, and serve two or three sauces with it. In a restaurant, I like to seize the opportunity to have *beurre blanc* or hollandaise sauce, as I find them troublesome to make, but there are many simple and delicious sauces that can be made quickly; I like a creamy horseradish sauce with fried fillets of a fish like sole, while a sorbet (water ice) of tomatoes and sour cream is quite delicious with *goujons* of sole. An herb sauce made with dill and tarragon or chervil is ideal with a poached white fish, while a béchamel made from fish stock and cream is far better than a cheese sauce in combined dishes. A curry sauce with white fish is excellent, as is saffron sauce. Herb butters cannot be improved upon; parsley butter is probably the best of all with broiled Dover sole, but more unusual butters can be made with tarragon or chervil.

Cold fish dishes are among my favorite summer choices. Fillets of poached fish in clear aspic with a light curry sauce make a good first course, as does a fish salad of poached halibut dressed with olive oil and lemon juice, and plenty of chopped herbs. Fillets of sole in a *chaudfroid* sauce garnished with tarragon leaves look pretty, while a cold fish mousse with a contrasting sauce makes a good main course for a light meal. I also have a passion for solid white fish like swordfish and pompano and I love the Mediterranean dishes of *loup de mer* and *daurade*, but Dover sole cannot be surpassed for delicacy of flavor and texture.

Halibut is one of my favorites too, because of its firm texture and excellent flavor. I like it cut in steaks and broiled, or baked in the oven with strips of bacon. Turbot is a close rival; this soft and delicate fish responds best to poaching, and the ideal accompaniment is hollandaise sauce. Bass is a nice firm fish, good served cold with tomatoes, onions and herbs. For a hot dish, it can be baked in the oven with bacon.

Sadly the oily fish like mackerel and sardines are only at their best when eaten within hours of being caught. Herrings are one of the cheapest and most nutritious of fish, yet are not prepared by many home cooks. It may be the bones that put people off; the only way I like them is filleted, coated in coarse oatmeal, brushed with melted butter and broiled.

I rarely buy cod except for two excellent dishes that demand it. One is cod with *aïoli*, a piece of cod poached and served with a wide variety of boiled vegetables and a garlicky sauce. The other is a less well-known Belgian dish of cod baked in the oven with butter and lemon juice; it is surprisingly good.

All dishes of hot poached fish are improved by the addition of steamed or boiled potatoes, particularly when they have a sauce. I find that little else is needed except perhaps a glass of good white wine.

16

Beachcombing

Take a stroll along the beach at low tide and discover a veritable wealth of delectable food: it is a true gourmet's paradise, and all for free

The seashore has been a rich hunting ground for scavengers since time began, especially during the winter months, when little nourishment was to be found on land. In the Hebrides, strange conical mounds were found near the shore which, on excavation, turned out to be the garbage dumps of the very earliest settlers, and furnished abundant proof that they lived entirely on the seashore. This was probably for two reasons: first as a source of food, and secondly as protection from the wild animals that inhabited the wooded interior. In the pits were found fossilized fish bones, bones of sea gulls, birds' eggs, and seashells, giving a clear picture of their diet.

The first English settlers in America likewise lived on food gathered from the beaches before they succeeded in penetrating inland and then cultivating the land.

Although I have spent part of almost every summer since I can remember by the sea, in one country or another, I have never been interested in this aspect of it until recently. During a week in Wales with my son, when we spent two days on the beaches, I was amazed by the abundance of food to be gathered. On an estuary in North Wales, equipped only with a child's bucket and spade, we had found enough food within a couple of hours to last us for a few days, had we been desperate. Three huge clams, each bigger than my fist, dozens of mussels clinging to the seaweed in clean rocky pools, cockles, and tiny crabs. Had we had a net we could have caught hundreds of tiny shrimps, and with luck some of a shoal of small fish which were jumping in a large pool. We also found two edible seaweeds.

I met an old man on the sands who told me how, as a boy, he used to catch as many fish as he wanted in the same place. He used a piece of strong string from twelve to eighteen feet long armed with steel hooks at intervals. These he would bait with sandworms, easily found by digging where little holes and worm casts appear side by side at low tide. Each end of the string was pegged firmly on the sand and left until the tide had risen and ebbed again, when he would return to find the hooks loaded with fish of various different sorts.

Shrimping has long been a favorite occupation both of those who live near the seashore and of vacationers. To net the sort of tiny transparent shrimps found in Britain, proper equipment is vital. So that they won't slip through as they dart about, the net must be of the finest possible mesh; it should be quite deep, with a flat end bound with wood, and a long handle. This is pushed through the shallows when the tide is

farthest out and when it is just on the turn. The shrimps are then transferred from the net to a bag that has a flap to keep them from jumping out; this is usually worn slung around the neck or waist. On getting home one flings them into swiftly boiling water, when they will immediately turn bright pink, and lets them cook for one minute. Shelling them is a very fiddly business for they are so small, but they are so delicious as to make it worthwhile.

Clams are also found at low tide, but a little earlier, when the tide is still receding. They lie under the surface of the sand, where their presence can be detected by holes, sometimes with jets of water spurting from them. Most of them can be eaten either raw or cooked, but the large ones we found in Wales would certainly have been too tough to eat raw.

Mussels can be found with no difficulty, clinging to pipes and piers, but they must not be eaten unless they come from clean water with no sewage outlets in the vicinity.

There are three main edible seaweeds that grow on the western shores of the British Isles. These are dulse (*Rhodymenia palmata*), carrageen (*Chondrus crispus*), and laver (*Porphyra umbilicalis* or *laciniata*). Dulse is a red algae, still occasionally eaten in parts of Scotland. Carrageen, or Irish moss, is usually dried and sold in health food shops. It is a natural form of gelatine, with little taste of its own, and rich in iodine and other minerals. It can be used as a thickening agent for soups or stews, or can even be employed for making sweet jellies or jams. After being carried home, it must be washed for several hours in fresh water, then laid out to bleach in the sun and, ideally, showers of rain, over a period of some days. When dry, it must be stored in a completely dry place or it will absorb moisture from the atmosphere.

Laver (called sloke in Ireland) is still made much use of in South Wales. It is a large brownish seaweed, almost transparent, which lies over the rocks like a fine net. It must be pulled from the rocks and washed for several hours, preferably in a mountain stream, then boiled for five or six hours, until it is reduced to a blackish pulp, slightly slimy in texture, like overcooked spinach. It can be bought in Wales in this form, referred to as "laver bread." It is then usually mixed with ground oatmeal to make flat cakes, which are fried in bacon fat. Cooked simply as a vegetable, with the juice of a bitter Seville orange, it is the traditional accompaniment to the delicious Welsh lamb, which can be seen grazing on the salt marshes alongside the beach.

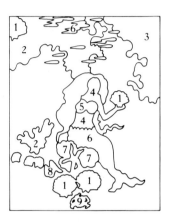

1 Scallops
2 Dulse
3 Gut laver
4 Shrimps
5 Prawns
6 Sprats
7 Oysters
8 Mussels
9 Crab

potted shrimps p87
barbecued shrimps p87
curried shellfish p87
tomato chili sauce p103
shrimp sauce p107

Chicken supreme

Whatever your mood or resources, chicken is endlessly adaptable. Hot or cold, mild or spicy, unadorned or in a creamy sauce, for picnics or parties, chicken reigns supreme

Since time immemorial, and in almost every culture, the chicken has found its way into the pot. In earlier times it was regarded as something of a luxury; a roast chicken was many families' Sunday treat, in preference to roast beef. The spread of factory farming has resulted in the general availability of cheap and tender birds, but there has been an inevitable deterioration in flavor. I bought a chicken in a small town in Tuscany recently and was horrified by its appearance. It was a terrible color with mottled orange flesh, huge misshapen legs, and bright yellow feet of vast size—not exactly high in "eye appeal." I bought it nonetheless and cooked it with a bunch of herbs from the garden and melted butter mixed with orange and lemon juice. It was the best tasting chicken I have eaten for a long time, in spite of the fact that I had neglected to remove its innards so that it took an amazingly long time to cook, a fact which gave great pleasure to the other cook in the household. ("Fancy writing about how to cook and not knowing enough to take the innards out of the chicken.") This shaming experience taught me two things: first, always to check the innards, and second, to make a point of buying farm-bred chickens from time to time to remind myself how a real bird can taste.

Any tender little fowl is eatable when broiled to a crisp golden brown, but a larger farm bird, cut in pieces and broiled, or roasted whole on a spit, is a far better dish. As a cook, I would be lost without chickens, for I find them one of the most versatile of foods. Their very lack of strong flavor means that they can be used as a vehicle for myriad different tastes, scents, and colors. They can be flavored with Oriental spices, with saffron or with mustard; they can be scented with fresh summer herbs, with tarragon, basil or thyme. They can be grilled over charcoal until crispy and almost charred, or poached and served in a delicate cream sauce. They can be stuffed with mixtures of bread crumbs, shallots and herbs, or with a layer of delicate farce, or forcemeat, like a mixture of sorrel and cream cheese (*à la cuisine minceur*) pushed between the skin and the flesh. Slices of black truffle are sometimes inserted in this way; the bird is then steamed in a chicken broth, and served with a velouté sauce. Chickens can be made into a spicy curry, or something bland like chicken à la king.

I prefer to cook a bird slowly in a covered casserole in the oven, with butter and lemon juice and a bunch of mixed herbs—marjoram, basil, rosemary and thyme.

Another chicken dish of which I am very fond is the Belgian *waterzooi*: a semi-liquid dish of neat fillets of chicken, covered by a thick sauce made from the many vegetables with which it has been poached, enriched with cream and egg yolks. I have a great affection for these sorts of dishes, a cross between a soup and a main dish, eaten in soup plates with knife, fork and spoon.

The tender flesh of the chicken combined with its crisp skin makes it ideal for barbecues, as it cooks quickly and is improved by a degree of intense heat to char the skin; thus it is also well suited to broiling and spit-roasting. It can be first marinated in a mixture of yogurt or oil and lemon juice, spices and herbs, or it can be simply painted with mustard and basted with olive oil and lemon juice. Boneless chicken can be cut in neat pieces, threaded on skewers, and basted with a mixture of melted butter, lemon juice and minced garlic. Drumsticks are excellent for picnics or barbecues where they are to be eaten in the fingers. I like to baste them with the same barbecue sauce I use for spareribs. The wings can be used in an elegant dish—a *chaudfroid* of chicken, or a *poulet à l'estragon*. The breasts alone can be fried in butter for a quick and simple dish.

A whole bird is best for a dish of chicken in aspic, or for a chicken pie, sometimes in small individual dishes, which I find very appetizing. One whole bird can be made into two related dishes; the best of the flesh can be cut up for skewers, for instance, while the carcass and scraps can be made into a most excellent soup, combined with young vegetables and rice or noodles. Chicken livers are useful as the basis for a quick pâté, or as an addition to a risotto. Last of all, the chicken gives us the most useful and delicate of stocks without which I would be lost. So many dishes depend on a good chicken stock, and prepared substitutes, though useful, are not really comparable.

Making more of lamb

Plain roast lamb is so good that few of us experiment further. Yet lamb has a natural affinity with many herbs, spices and vegetables which should on no account go unexplored

English lamb is probably the best in the world, yet apart from the admittedly delicious roast leg of lamb, and broiled lamb cutlets, surprisingly little use is made of it. There is no British equivalent, for example, to that most delicious of all casseroles the *navarin d'agneau*, in which tender lamb is simmered in broth with a variety of tiny vegetables, each added to the pot at carefully graduated intervals so that all are tender at the same moment. In England, there is no understanding of dishes like *boeuf bourguignon*, in which beef is cooked slowly in good red wine to make a really delicious meal. A friend, who is a good and inventive cook, once said sadly that when she had spent hours simmering a chicken in bouillon with myriad different vegetables, her husband would simply look in the pot and say, "Oh, stew again." A saddle of lamb is the best of all cuts for roasting, but one can roast a piece of the same animal in a smaller and less expensive form, in the cut the French call *carré d'agneau*. The English term for this is a rack of lamb, and it usually consists of seven bones; this will serve three people, or four at a pinch. In many good American restaurants, a six-bone carré is served for two people, and carved lengthwise like a saddle of lamb, in thin strips. The bones are cut up and served separately.

A shoulder of lamb is a cut I like immensely. Cheaper than the leg, it is more fatty and not really suitable for roasting. I like to braise it with lots of vegetables and serve it with a sauce made from the cooking liquid enriched with a roux or egg yolks. It is also excellent cooked slowly in the oven and served on a bed of haricot beans well flavored with garlic.

In the country, I cook a boned leg of lamb on a rack over the fire; the only drawback is the shrinkage, for the flavor is extraordinary. I tried doing this in London recently, starting it off under the broiler and finishing in the oven. It was almost as good, and took only thirty-five minutes to cook a large leg. The secret is to get your butcher to cut out the bone in such a way that you are left with a rectangular slab of meat, roughly even in thickness. Another good way of cooking a boned leg, and even quicker, is to treat it like a steak and serve with parsley butter. Ask the butcher to cut out the bone leaving the meat as intact as possible: then you need only cut it across in thick slices, as many as you need, brush with olive oil and lemon juice, and broil.

In the Middle East almost all the meat dishes are made from lamb, for beef is almost non-existent. *Moussaka*, for instance, meatballs, and *kafta*—rolls of ground meat pressed around skewers and broiled—are all far more tasty when made with lamb, which seems to have a greater affinity with spices than beef. It certainly goes admirably with the other Middle Eastern accompaniments, the salads of chopped herbs and cracked wheat, and the dishes of cucumber in yogurt. I think the best of all skewered dishes is the Greek *souvlakia*, tiny pieces of lamb threaded on thin sticks, marinated in oil and lemon juice, broiled and served three or four to each person. Nothing else is added—no leaves, onion rings or halved tomatoes—and with the accompaniment of hot pita bread, *tsatsiki* and the inevitable Greek salad, this is a meal of which I never tire. In doner kebab establishments, huge mounds of lamb, revolving vertically on a spit, are carved downwards in thin strips and stuffed into steaming hot pita to make a delicous meat sandwich, an Eastern form of hamburger.

Finally, I like lamb cold, with a mint sauce made with lemon juice instead of vinegar, or perhaps apple and quince jelly. When accompanied by a salad it makes an impressive and delicious summer meal.

1 *Braised shoulder of lamb with vegetables*
2 *Sauce for braised lamb*
3 *Spicy meatballs*
4 *Mint sauce*
5 *Stuffed eggplant*
6 *Carré d'agneau*
7 *Yogurtlyia*
8 *Pita bread*
9 *Souvlakia*
10 *Quince jelly*

$\mathcal{S}$ ubstantial salads

Shellfish, poultry, nuts, fruits, cheese, crisp fresh vegetables—combine whatever you choose and create a colorful salad that makes a wholesome meal in itself

1 *Shellfish salad*
2 *Rosemary; mint*
3 *Prawns*
4 *Scallops*
5 *Chives*
6 *Garlic*

When I have had occasion to prepare elaborate meals, it has always annoyed me that I did not have enough time to spend on the salad. There were always other more important things to attend to. Now, for a variety of reasons, I like to take one thing which used to be considered as a mere part of the meal, a detail, and by spending a lot of care and thought on it, turn it into a meal in itself. I started to do this with cooked vegetable dishes; now I do it with salads. A salad can be a whole meal in microcosm; it may contain meat, poultry, fish, cheese, eggs, nuts, fruits, olives, a huge variety of vegetables, raw and cooked, and even bread, or croutons.

A fairly substantial salad seems to me a perfect lunch. Even if I am alone, I almost always have a meal of some sort in the middle of the day; I find it as hard to work all afternoon on an empty stomach as I do after a large lunch with half a bottle of wine. A salad is the obvious answer— not a simple green salad, which would be my first choice if eaten as an accompaniment to another dish— but a *salade composée*, that is to say, a salad made up of a mixture of ingredients, some cooked, some raw—like a salade niçoise.

I love these sorts of dishes: light, appetizing, and nutritious; they are neither too expensive nor troublesome to make. During the summer months a salad of this sort, accompanied by a crusty loaf of bread and followed by some homemade yogurt, makes a perfect light meal. In colder weather, for a more sustaining meal, it can be accompanied by a hot soup, or perhaps a ramekin of eggs baked in the oven.

I refuse to give up eating certain foods just because they have become too expensive, but I don't mind eating them less often, and in smaller quantities. Another advantage of these sorts of salads is that they are a good way of using small amounts of costly materials, and making them into a proper dish. Shellfish has become too expensive for most of us to contemplate buying in large quantities but we can still afford a few crawfish or lobster tails or a handful of prawns or shrimps occasionally. Quite apart from the expense, it is important that the "solid" part of the dish be kept down in relation to the leafy content, or the dish will change its character entirely. I remember reading a stricture of Elizabeth David's years ago, about not overfilling an omelette; two tablespoons was, I think, all she would allow for a three-egg omelette—and I realize now how right she was. A similar formula could be adopted for salads.

Although a salad is by its nature a mixture of things, it must be a carefully chosen mixture, not just a heap of leftovers. The cooked part must be freshly cooked, and should be either just one thing or a group of closely related things: a mixture of shellfish, for example, or a combination of new vegetables. There are a few exceptions: hard-boiled eggs go well with fish, or with a mixture of cooked vegetables; crisp bacon and mozzarella cheese make a delicious combination with finely shredded summer spinach and sliced avocado. The ingredients should be cut in similar-sized pieces; whereas in a simple lettuce salad I leave the leaves whole, in a mixed salad of this sort I usually cut them in manageable strips.

As far as I am concerned, a salad is composed mainly of raw vegetables, most of them green and leafy: raw spinach or sorrel, lettuce, endive, chicory, watercress, cucumber and radishes. The numerous Italian dishes of cooked vegetables dressed with oil and lemon are sometimes called salads, but, good as they are, they do not really fit into this category.

Lastly there is the choice of dressings. With an elaborate salad, one containing chicken or fish, I think the best solution is to have two dressings: one very simple to mix with the dish itself beforehand; the other quite different, more of a sauce, creamy and quite thick, which is handed around at the table. If a thick sauce of this type is poured over the salad it spoils the appearance and gives a slightly gluey consistency; another advantage in keeping it separate is that those on a diet can avoid the richer sauce altogether. With a shellfish salad, for instance, I would cook the fish and marinate it in lemon juice for an hour before serving, then I would dress the assembled salad with the best olive oil and more lemon juice. When serving, I would have a mayonnaise in a separate bowl. With a chicken salad, I would marinate the pieces of cooked chicken briefly in lemon juice, then dress the assembled salad with a light oil (like sunflower seed oil) and more lemon; I would accompany it with a creamy herb sauce flavored with fresh tarragon or dill.

With the salads containing dried bread, cheese or nuts, a creamy sauce is not wanted, but with salads of mixed cooked vegetables, or of hard-boiled eggs, it can be an optional extra. The addition of the second sauce will serve to turn the whole dish into something more special, quite elegant enough for a lunch party, and even for a light summer dinner party.

Mouthwatering salads

Light, moist, cool, alluring and properly dressed to enhance their flavor, salads can be as ravishing to the eye as they are appealing and appetizing to the palate

Descriptions of salads in books always make my mouth water. The other day I came across an account of a meal the author had eaten at Sissinghurst including "a delicious salad of watercress, orange sections, chopped shallots, with a little orange in the lemon oil dressing." I couldn't wait to try it, for it seemed to promise just the quality of salad which I love, and it proved worthy of its description.

Whereas the French and Italian *salade composée*, a dish of cooked vegetables in a vinaigrette, can be a meal in itself, raw salads make a perfect accompaniment to many main dishes. To me, green leaves and fruity vegetables—tomatoes, avocados, cucumbers and peppers—make up some of the most appealing as well as the most nutritious of dishes. My favorite among salads is made from the thinnings of the rows of salad vegetables in my own garden. A mixture of tender young leaves of lettuce, sorrel, spinach, mustard and dandelion, this salad is very similar to some I have eaten in Italy, made of wild salad greens gathered in the fields, lightly dressed.

I like to make each salad dressing to suit the individual salad, and with the rest of the meal in mind. With a tender salad of thinnings, I usually make a dressing out of a light oil like sunflower seed oil, a few drops of lemon juice, a light sprinkling of black pepper and a pinch of sugar. With a more robust mixture of leaves, perhaps including watercress, endive or chicory, I would use olive oil, white wine vinegar, garlic, sea salt, sugar, black pepper and Dijon mustard. I usually mix the dressing in the empty salad bowl while the leaves stand in their drainer. When fresh herbs are available, I chop them at the last moment, just before tossing the salad. If added earlier to flavor the dressing, they lose their bright color, which is part of their appeal. My favorite mixture is equal parts of tarragon, chervil and chives; I also use each of these singly or mixed with parsley. With tomato salads I prefer

basil alone, while with cucumber salads I use dill, chervil, burnet or mint. The only dried herb I use is oregano, which adds a Mediterranean flavor, and is particularly good with salads containing avocado, tomatoes or mozzarella.

The choice of oils and vinegars is wide. I usually have a large can of light-flavored Italian olive oil, a fruitier green "virgin" oil from Tuscany, French arachide oil, sunflower seed oil and a small can of walnut oil. For the most part I use the light olive oil, with the more highly flavored Tuscan oil as alternative. In early autumn I make a salad with fresh green walnuts, using the curious walnut oil. For the acid element I use white wine vinegar or lemon juice, or a mixture of the two. I also have a selection of homemade herb vinegars. The four best ones are those flavored with burnet, shallot, basil and garlic together, and garlic alone.

One of the most important aspects of a dish is the visual one, as anyone who has eaten Japanese food is well aware. Scallions, radishes and celery can be carved into exquisite shapes and left in a bowl of ice water in the refrigerator overnight, to create a ravishing effect. A small amount of food beautifully arranged on a plate is more appealing than a huge quantity of food whatever the dish. For me the prettiest salads are a mixture of greens, ranging from the dark watercress to the pale ice-green of peeled cucumber. I also love a mixture of green and white with a little red, which is supplied by thinly sliced radishes, or finely chopped tomato.

But after all, probably the best salad is lettuce alone, with a simple dressing. I agree with June Platt, who says in her *Plain and Fancy Cookbook*: "Best of all I like a plain green salad with a well-seasoned French dressing, eaten, not as a separate course, but as a sole accompaniment to the hot roast chicken or roast veal, the clear syrupy gravy mixing with the salad on the plate being my idea of a heavenly dish."

1 Radishes
2 Scallions
3 Carrot
4 Celery

$\mathcal{A}$ bouquet of herbs

Fresh, fragrant, subtle or pervasive, herbs have always been praised for their magical, medicinal and culinary properties and are today indispensable to the creative cook

1 *Lovage*
2 *Angelica*
3 *Marjoram*
4 *Basil*
5 *Fennel*
6 *Chives*
7 *Good King Henry*
8 *Tarragon*
9 *Orach*
10 *Garlic*
11 *Pennyroyal*
12 *Hyssop*
13 *Sage*
14 *Rosemary*
15 *Thyme*
16 *Summer savory*
17 *Purslane*
18 *Pineapple mint*
19 *Eau de cologne mint*
20 *Peppermint*
21 *Apple mint*
22 *Spearmint*
23 *Lemon balm*
24 *Borage*

Reading through early cookbooks, one is constantly reminded of the important part herbs played in early English domestic life. Every manor house and monastery had its own herb garden, many of them very large indeed, and it was not until the sixteenth century that the separate flower garden was conceived. This was mainly due to the immigrants from Flanders, fleeing from Spanish persecution, who carried with them advanced methods of cultivation, as well as many new fruits, flowers and vegetables.

For several centuries before that, the herb garden had reigned supreme. The meaning of the word "herb" then was loose, and large herb gardens included many plants we do not now think of in that context. Webster's gives as a meaning: "a plant or plant part valued for its medicinal, savory or aromatic qualities."

According to this definition the wide range of plants grown in many of the fourteenth- and fifteenth-century herb gardens was perfectly correct, for each had its special use. There were onions, leeks, garlic, lettuce, beets, nettles, sorrel, radishes and spinach; also roses, lilies, peonies, carnations (known as gilly-flowers), violets, mallows, primroses, marigolds, honeysuckle, lavender and daisies.

The usual form of herb garden—that of an enclosed rectangular plot laid out in geometric form—has descended from the old monastic herb gardens, which were usually surrounded with high banks of earth walls or tall hedges.

A modern English garden is also an extension of this plan, with its herbaceous borders—the word "herb" in this context meaning any plant whose stem dies down after flowering, i.e. a perennial.

The history of herbs goes farther back than the earliest English records, for they are among the most ancient of plants; many of them were known to the ancient Persians and Egyptians, Greeks and Romans. The Egyptians put bunches of herbs in the hands of their mummies, and in the fourth century BC Hippocrates compiled a list of four hundred herbs relating to matters of health. The Romans were responsible for introducing many of their favorite herbs to the British Isles, such as chives, parsley, rosemary, chervil and sage. After the departure of the Romans, the cultivation of herbs was taken over by the monasteries. Yet there must have been some knowledge of herbs in Britain even before Roman times, for they were used by the Druids, who performed ceremonies of propitiation before

picking them. As Christianity ousted these practices, the monks substituted prayers for the earlier incantations. Some of these still survive and are very beautiful, but it is sad that their pagan antecedents were destroyed. As modern life, with its insistence on common sense, took over, the magical qualities of herbs were forgotten, although some of their mystery still persists in the beliefs, strongly held although hard to prove, of their curing powers.

As flavoring for food, herbs have been neglected in Britain, despite this long history. At friends' or in restaurants, I rarely have the pleasure of eating dishes where the herb is an intrinsic part, as opposed to a mere garnish. Classic British dishes are poor in this respect, in comparison with those of other countries; we have little to offer on a par with the French *poulet à l'estragon*, or *jambon persillé*, or the Provençal *pistou*. The Belgians have their *anguilles au vert*, the Italians their *salsa verde*, their pizzas aromatic with oregano, and their many dishes of veal flavored with sage or rosemary. In the Middle Eastern countries there are salads of parsley and mint, sauces made from *tahini* and parsley, and dishes of cucumber in yogurt lavishly seasoned with dried mint.

The greatest value of herbs, in my opinion, is for the creative cook. Herbs lend themselves to imaginative treatment, and once one understands an herb and its affinities, it is hard to go wrong. Among my favorites for cooking are basil and tarragon, chervil and dill.

Basil is delicious with tomatoes, eggs and vegetable dishes; tarragon is at its best used with chicken or eggs. Chervil is like a subtler, more delicate form of parsley, and is one of the best herbs for mixing with other herbs. I am especially fond of dill, combined with mustard in a creamy sauce for boiled beef or chicken, with hard-boiled eggs, boiled potatoes, cucumber or beets.

I like to have two or three varieties of mint in my herb garden: spearmint for cooking, apple mint for its pretty variegated leaf, and eau-de-cologne, or pineapple mint, for its delicious scent.

If I were now starting grown-up life, as I did twenty years ago, in a small house with a tiny rectangular south-facing garden plot, I could think of no better use for it than as an herb garden. Herbs will flourish in the poorest of soils so long as they get plenty of sun, and with the addition of a glass frame even more delicate varieties like basil, which needs heat to develop its true flavor, could be grown successfully.

The first vegetable harvest

In spring, vegetables are in the prime of their youth. Enjoy them at their best—raw or lightly steamed, unaccompanied or with a variety of tasty dips and sauces

Unlike animal foods, vegetables gain little by being allowed to reach maturity. In almost every case they are at their best when small, with a fully developed flavor and a firm, crisp texture. As often happens, the French have a term for these young vegetables which describes them exactly: *les primeurs*. This means literally "the first," in other words the first of the season, not out-of-season produce taken from cold storage.

The younger the vegetable, the more it has to lose by being long out of the ground. No early vegetable keeps well; even early potatoes do not have the keeping properties of the later varieties. In English country houses there used to be running battles between the cook and the head gardener, for their aims were diametrically opposed. The cook was crying out for young vegetables, while the gardener could not resist growing each one to its proper size. Needless to say, this is a problem that few of us have to face nowadays; those lucky enough to be both cook and gardener will see the advantages.

When very young, vegetables are best treated as simply as possible. We should keep for later the soufflés, purees, quiches and vinaigrettes.

Preparing *crudités* is a matter of presentation, not cooking. What one needs is a pleasing combination of very fresh young vegetables which complement each other in color and in texture, and a pretty platter on which to serve them. After being cleaned scrupulously, they should be chilled briefly in the refrigerator, then cut into appropriate shapes and arranged prettily, perhaps on a bed of crushed ice. One or two complementary sauces, thick enough for dipping, should be served at the same time. This makes a perfect start to a summer luncheon. A similar method of presentation can be applied to a selection of spring vegetables which have been very lightly cooked, just enough to render them more digestible, and served while still warm. Scallions, for instance, are delicious cooked briefly with their green part still on and served with steamed snow peas and mushrooms, accompanied by a garlicky mayonnaise. A number of good sauces can be made from combinations of cream cheese with yogurt or sour cream, with chopped herbs or tomato puree

added. These are quickly made in a blender.

The cooking of young vegetables is best done by one of the following methods. First, by boiling in the minimum of lightly salted water for the shortest possible time, just long enough to soften them slightly without losing their firmness, then draining and tossing them in melted butter; the butter should not be allowed to overheat or change its color. Second, they can be steamed, which suits most vegetables with the possible exception of green beans, which lose some of their intense color. Here again the timing is vital, for if left a moment too long they develop an unpleasant taste. My third suggestion may seem strange, but I cannot recommend it too highly. It is to cook whole vegetables, even the youngest, in a pressure cooker. It works remarkably well, especially with zucchini. The timing varies from two to four minutes, and is learned after one or two careful experiments.

Special pans for steaming can be bought, but I like the gadget in stainless steel which opens out like the petals of a flower to fit almost any saucepan. The Chinese wicker steamers are pretty and easy to use, especially if you have a wok over which to stack them. I love the old-fashioned French pots for steaming potatoes, in shiny brown china, but they are fragile. Steamed potatoes are far superior to boiled peeled potatoes, especially for eating with fish or any dish with a delicate sauce. Sprigs of dill can be laid among them as they steam, and salt added after cooking. Young vegetables are best steamed over plain water, although older root vegetables may benefit from cooking over a meat stock.

May and June are the best of all months for eating young vegetables, even the root vegetables which we associate with winter. I have always loved a whole course of vegetables. Three or four served on one plate can be delicious after a cold first course, or a hot fish which is best eaten alone. In this way they can take the place of the salad which often follows a hot meat dish. I usually prefer to keep each vegetable separate, but later in the season I often mix three together—green beans, carrots and zucchini, for example—in a béchamel made from the cooking liquor enriched with cream.

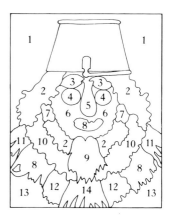

| 1 Cabbage leaves |
| 2 Carrots |
| 3 Broad beans; peppers; red cabbage |
| 4 Onions |
| 5 Eggplant |
| 6 Tomatoes |
| 7 Red peppers |
| 8 Broad beans; peas |
| 9 Fennel |
| 10 Cauliflower |
| 11 Runner beans; broad beans |
| 12 Red cabbage |
| 13 Spinach |
| 14 Onion tops |

tomato sauce 3 p103
garlic mayonnaise p104
pistou p106
mustard sauce p106
horseradish sauce p107
green sauce p107

$\mathcal{A}$ litany of leaves

Sorrel, rocket, Good King Henry, purslane, corn salad, orach, chard, mustard leaves, watercress, dandelion, buttercrunch, ruby beet and curly kale

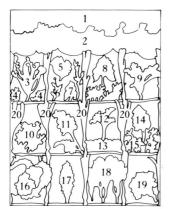

Three hundred years ago, many more salad vegetables were grown in Great Britain than nowadays. In a cookbook of the period the first chapter is devoted to salads: they are rated "of the first importance." But many of the vegetables therein have been forgotten by the British, although some of them are still widely used on the continent.

Rocket, for example, once grew so widely in England that it threatened to overrun the City of London after the great fire of 1666. It has remained popular in Italy, where it is known as *rucola*, *rugola*, or *rucetta*. It has a strong, rather bitter taste, and is thought to have medicinal qualities; I think it is best added to a green salad in small amounts. Though it is scarce in markets, its seeds are easily obtainable, and growing it presents no problem.

Dandelion leaves are popular in France and Italy. Good King Henry, or Mercury, is an old English plant, similar to spinach, that is still found in markets in France. Purslane is another good vegetable that has fallen into disuse. These days I only see it in Greece, but it can be bought from many Greek-Cypriot shops, although not by that name. It is easily recognized by its fat juicy stem with a rosette of round green leaves at the top. It can be used in salads, or cooked in the Greek way with eggs. Corn salad is also much more common in France, where it is called *mâche*. Orach has been forgotten everywhere, yet this pretty plant with heart-shaped leaves of red and green is easily grown. It is cooked like spinach, and tastes like a mixture of spinach and sorrel. Those with a liking for slightly bitter leaves should look for the red-leafed lettuce called *trevigiana* in Italy. Milder than rocket, it looks very pretty when mixed with a green lettuce salad.

Those with their own gardens should try growing mustard, not for the yellow flowers but for the young leaves, which have a hot, peppery taste delicious in a mixed green salad. And even in a small garden, a few rows of unusual lettuces are well worth growing. Sorrel is also worth having; even a small handful of sorrel leaves will give a lift to a dish of cooked spinach or a salad.

The young leaves of summer spinach also make a good raw salad, especially when combined with crisply fried bits of bacon, with their hot fat replacing the usual oil in the dressing. Other good combinations with spinach are sliced raw mushrooms, avocado and mozzarella cheese. The older leaves are better cooked; they can be served alone or made into soups or quiches.

Even easier to grow than spinach is spinach beet, for it has an apparent resistance to frost. Basically a tougher form of spinach with a well-developed central stem, it is much used in France, where it is called *bettes*. There are many varieties: sea-kale beet, chard, ruby beet and ruby chard. In the case of chard the central stem is the main point of the plant, and is cooked like sea-kale. In others, where the leaf and the stem are equally well developed, they can be cooked together while still very young, but if picked later on, are best cooked separately. The leaves can be treated like spinach, while the stems should be cut in thick chunks and will require about five minutes' longer cooking time.

Watercress is widely grown in England, but for some reason it is considered a garnish and rarely cooked. It is rich in minerals and vitamins and I love its peppery taste. I use it often, in hot and cold soups, in salads, in sauces for soft-boiled eggs in the summer, or as a substitute for mint sauce during the winter.

Chinese cabbage is a recent import to Great Britain, although it has figured in Chinese cooking for centuries. It is like a cross between a lettuce and a green cabbage. It is good either cooked or raw, and is useful for stuffed cabbage dishes, for the leaves combine the size and strength of cabbage with the delicacy of lettuce.

The magic of mushrooms

The wildest of wild foods, the most mysterious and magical, mushrooms can be cooked in so many imaginative ways or eaten raw in salads or sandwiches

"If red mullet are the 'woodcock of the sea' on account of their delicate taste, mushrooms might be called the 'oysters of the fields', for no other food has quite the rare flavor of these elfin-like mysteries that grow by the light of the moon, or, to be more accurate, in darkness."

So wrote Mrs Leyel in her enchanting book *The Gentle Art of Cookery*, first published in 1925. She goes on to suggest using a silver spoon in the cooking, as a way to guard against poisonous fungi; in the case of inedible varieties the spoon will turn black, she says. I would not place much confidence in this, or in other ways of distinguishing between safe fungi and their alarmingly similar poisonous cousins. The only one I feel totally confident about is the common field mushroom, which is also my favorite. Where I live, surrounded by woods, they are rarely found, for they prefer to grow on open land in meadows and pastures. The fungi that grow under trees are altogether more exotic, more colorful and more dangerous. The ones in the photograph were all gathered one morning in the New Forest by Tessa Traeger, and were later identified as safe by the British Museum's Natural History staff. Even so, I would not recommend using the picture as a guide, for it is not worth taking risks.

Mushrooms are to me the wildest of wild foods, the most mysterious and magical. I used to find it hard to understand how they could spring up so rapidly, with a life cycle only slightly longer than that of the butterfly, and of what tissue they could be made, that grew and died away so quickly. I have now learned that what we call the mushroom is in fact only one of the external growths of the full mushroom, which is a mass of tangled spores below the surface of the ground. These growths are brought on, at variable distances, by climatic conditions.

I once ate a mushroom as big as a soup plate in a restaurant in Parma. It was a local specialty, which literally covered the whole plate and tasted like the reduced essence of every wild mushroom that ever grew.

For those who feel squeamish about unusual fungi, there is always the cultivated variety, which can be bought all year round. Mushrooms are a good source of nourishment despite their rapid growth, in that they contain a high amount of vitamin D and very few calories. On the other hand, they act like blotting paper in cooking, and will absorb huge quantities of butter or oil. For those on diets, they can be broiled without fat, or simmered in stock. They can also be steamed.

Mushrooms should never be peeled, but rather wiped with a damp cloth, for most of the flavor lies in their skin. The stems are tougher than the caps and should be left out of delicate dishes; they can be used for flavoring stocks and sauces.

My favorite way of cooking mushrooms is to put them (whole, sliced or chopped) in a small pan with a piece of butter and a little lemon juice, and stew them gently, covered, for about 12 minutes, shaking the pan from time to time, until they are soft and tender and have made a delicious juice. They are also good deep-fried, the caps only, dipped into batter and fried for a few minutes in very hot oil, then served with deep-fried parsley and a tart mayonnaise.

Mushrooms, so long as they are very fresh, are good eaten raw. Dressed with plenty of olive oil and lemon juice, raw mushrooms either alone or combined with shredded raw spinach, sorrel or romaine, make a fine salad. They also make an unusually good sandwich. Cooked mushrooms are an excellent filling for savory pastries. Crisp fried bacon makes a particularly good contrast to their bland flavor, which also combines well with spinach and tomatoes. Mushrooms have an affinity too, with onions, shallots and garlic; and most herbs complement them, especially tarragon, dill, chervil, and parsley. In winter and summer alike they can be made into delicious soups and sauces, and they go well with chicken, fish, beef and lamb.

Wild mushrooms take slightly longer to cook than the cultivated ones; I usually stew them gently in butter in a frying pan, adding finely minced onion, garlic and herbs. The more delicate field mushroom does not need strong flavoring; the onion and garlic can be omitted and some cream added at the end. Dried mushrooms, usually a variety of *cep* or *boletus*, are to be soaked for two to four hours before using (the water can then be used as a light stock). They have a good flavor, and as they store well, they are a useful item to remember when stocking the larder.

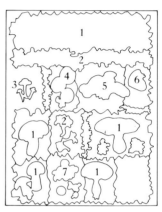

1 *Ceps*
2 *Chanterelles*
3 *Non-edible fungus*
4 *Field mushrooms*
5 *Oyster mushroom*
6 *Beefsteak mushroom*
7 *Puff balls*

A glut in the vegetable garden

Rows of bolted lettuce, a greenhouse full of overripe tomatoes and beds of elderly squash are a dread sight for the gardener and a challenge for the cook

1 Peas in pods
2 Spring onions
3 Variegated lemon balm, radishes, sage leaves
4 Gooseberries, parsley, chives
5 Dill leaves
6 Variegated lemon balm
7 Zucchini
8 Cucumber
9 Tomatoes
10 Broad beans
11 Turnips
12 Carrots
13 Sage
14 Green pepper
15 Rhubarb
16 Dill tops
17 Beets
18 Apple mint
19 Lettuce
20 Radish
21 Spinach leaf
22 Spearmint
23 Ginger mint

lettuce puree p98
spiced zucchini p99
fresh pease pudding p102
black currant leaf
  sorbet p113

Even in the smallest garden, high summer tends to produce a glut. Every gardener is only too familiar with the dread sight of the zucchini that got away, yet another vast squash skulking under its own large leaf like a plump Eve trying to hide behind her fig leaf. Lettuces start to go to seed *en masse*, for however carefully one tries to stagger the sowing, a spell of hot weather tends to bring them on together anyway. My efforts to avoid wastage by eating lettuces past their prime reminds me of my Scottish grandmother, who used to irritate my father inordinately by always insisting on eating the bruised peach each evening at the dinner table. He used to try to convince her, but in vain, that if she would only ignore it just once, it would be thrown away, and each evening thereafter she could have a perfect peach. I now feel rather the same about lettuce, for the very fact that some have bolted means that there are others about to bolt, and only by relegating a few of the worst to the compost heap can one hope to catch up. In fact, although they produce a bitter taste when eaten raw, overly mature lettuces can be cooked quite successfully; even their stalks can be boiled and eaten with melted butter.

Most of us can be divided somewhat summarily into Marthas or Marys by our habits. When it comes to coping with garden produce, I am most definitely a Mary. The Marthas are never caught out; nothing is allowed to spoil in their well-run gardens, for they simply rush out and spend hour after tedious hour picking, blanching and packaging for their vast freezers. I have a deep resistance to freezing fresh vegetables, probably because it bores me. Instead, I try to use as much as I can by making dishes to be eaten straight away, or in a few days; luckily nothing much is wasted because my garden is so minute. I prefer to use my freezer—also miniscule—for special things: young black currant leaves for making sorbets later in the summer, red and white currants in tiny bags for garnishing the same sorbets and other fruit desserts, and little bunches of my favorite summer herbs. I am convinced that the freezing of fresh vegetables only makes economic sense when done on a large scale, and for those of us who work in other ways this is just not practical, since our time is also valuable. This concept does not keep me from doing things I enjoy, like cooking some time-consuming dishes, but it certainly comes in handy when faced with tasks I dislike!

Zucchini squash should really be picked when no larger than a man's fingers, with the flowers still clinging to them, but they are still perfectly eatable when larger. If they cannot be eaten at once, they will stay crisp for about a week in the refrigerator, but they lose their delicious earthy taste within hours of being picked.

Many of the midsummer vegetables make delicious gratins, fillings for quiches, or soups. For the latter they can be used alone or in combination with added chicken stock, buttermilk, milk or cream. Some of the more unusual herbs and vegetables can be made into purees and frozen in small cartons for future use; sorrel and spinach are two of my favorites.

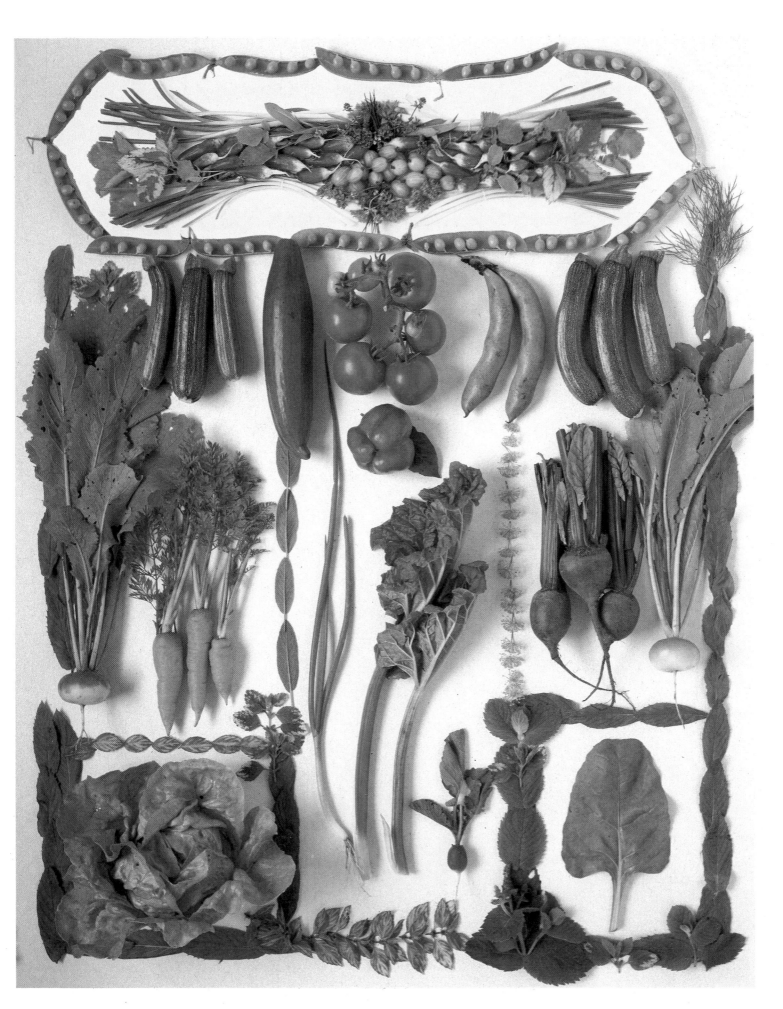

35

Midsummer vegetables

With all the flavor of exotic lands and the charm of foods ripened in the hot sun, midsummer vegetables share a Gallic affinity with olive oil, garlic and each other

There is a group of vegetables which is so closely related to fruit that it is hard to tell where one ends and the other begins. These are the juicy midsummer vegetables, the tomatoes and eggplants, the peppers in all their various shapes and colors; the cucumber, zucchini and other squashes, the giant pumpkins and decorative gourds; and the avocado.

They have the charm of foods that ripen in hot sun, with a flavor of the Mediterranean and other even more exotic lands. They contain fewer vitamins than leaf vegetables, for their water content is high, but they are nonetheless delicious for that. The exception is the avocado, which is strictly speaking a fruit, but a most unusual one in that it contains vast amounts of protein and of fat. It is extremely nourishing, but is best avoided by those on diets. The other members of this group are suitable for diets, except the eggplant, which absorbs large quantities of oil in cooking.

Apart from the avocado, the other vegetables in this group have much in common; they share an affinity with olive oil, garlic, and each other. None of them should be cooked in water, for they already contain so much. Zucchini can be parboiled briefly before broiling as a gratin, or before being cooled for a vinaigrette. They are frequently fried, whole or in slices, in shallow fat or deep oil, in which case they are first coated in batter or simply dipped in seasoned flour.

An elegant midsummer dish to serve is a hot platter of mixed vegetable fritters: eggplant, zucchini and tomatoes dipped in a light batter and fried in deep oil, and served with *skordalia*, the Greek garlic sauce, or simply with lemons. Green peppers are good either raw, in salads, or cooked in garlic and oil in dishes such as *piperade* or ratatouille. Canned red peppers are extremely good, and are useful for combining with tomatoes in certain Provençal dishes. Skinning fresh peppers is a time-consuming business, although it can be done by charring them all over under the broiler or over a gas flame.

Cucumbers are not often cooked, but in fact they can be substituted for zucchini in many recipes and are very good. Many squash of different shapes which are found in the United States are not known in England. One exception is the round tart-shaped one we call custard marrow. Their shells make pretty dishes for stuffing with rice and ground meat, or for baking small soufflés. As far as flavor is concerned, however, I much prefer the small zucchini, which we call courgette. Its larger relative, vegetable marrow, is best used for stuffing for it tends to be watery. It can be good, though, peeled and cut in chunks and stewed gently in butter in a lidded sauté pan, with some peeled and roughly chopped tomatoes added halfway through the cooking time. Fresh basil or marjoram improves this simple dish enormously.

Eggplants, which we call aubergines, are almost always fried in oil before being combined with other foods. They can be broiled whole or baked in the oven; broiling in particular gives a delicious smoky taste. Eggplants and tomatoes go well together, particularly if the tomatoes have the strong, sharp yet sweet flavor they acquire in really hot countries. Having to use tomatoes raised in the English climate, I sometimes find it best to drain away the seeds and juice and replace it with a little canned Italian tomato juice.

A delicious dish is made with layers of fried eggplant, onion, and tomatoes, baked in the oven with sliced mozzarella cheese melting over the top. I ate this regularly one summer in a little restaurant in Morocco, where the tomatoes are really splendid, and it has remained a firm favorite with me ever since.

Hot chili peppers are delicious but must be used with caution. They are very strong indeed, and only one, or two at the most, should be used in any dish. If they are to be part of an uncooked dish, like *guacamole* for instance, some of their fiery hotness will be taken away if they are first dropped into boiling water for two minutes. They must be carefully cleaned, for if any of the white seeds are left they will scorch the roof of your mouth. Added to curries, these little chili peppers give a lovely fresh hot taste, as opposed to the dry hotness of the spices.

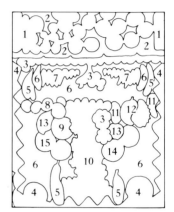

1 *Marrow squash*
2 *Zucchini squash*
3 *Tomatoes*
4 *Watermelon*
5 *Eggplant*
6 *Cucumbers*
7 *Chili peppers*
8 *Squashes*
9 *Yellow honeydew melon*
10 *Peppers*
11 *Avocado*
12 *Soursop (custard apple)*
13 *Mangoes*
14 *Ogen melon*
15 *Musk melon*

Berries, cherries and currants

Enticing desserts made from succulent strawberries, raspberries and currants are as much a part of summer as the lazy drone of bees and the clink of ice in tall glasses

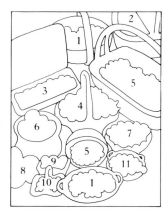

1 Black currants
2 Green gooseberries
3 Blueberries
4 Strawberries
5 White currants
6 Dessert gooseberries
7 Raspberries
8 Kiwi fruit (Chinese gooseberries)
9 Loganberries
10 Wild strawberries
11 Red currants

In summer, the café windows in Florence and other Italian towns are lined with rows of large glass goblets, filled to the brim with cut strawberries. These delicious looking *coppe* are served with scoops of ice cream in mouth-watering colors, with dollops of whipped cream or simply with lemon juice. Since so much of the pleasure of such fruits lies in their appearance, it seems sensible to display them in this way at home too, as often as possible.

Raspberries are so fragile that they are best treated with greater care. I think they look prettiest served piled on a lining of vine leaves in a shallow basket, with a slab of fresh cream cheese on a separate dish, and cream and sugar. Except in ice cream, jam and the pureed dessert called a "fool," cooked strawberries are disappointing, but cooked raspberries lend a delicious tart flavor to many dishes.

Raspberries combine well with red and white currants, and make a good tart when simply piled into a prebaked tart shell and warmed through in the oven. Strawberries can be treated in this way; in this case care should be taken that neither fruit is actually cooked.

Red and white currants are not widely grown in the United States, and American visitors to England think of them as truly "English." I rarely cook them, preferring to make them into uncooked desserts. They can be folded into mixtures of beaten egg whites, cream and yogurt flavored with vanilla sugar, for a pretty, light dessert, or used to cover a meringue beneath a covering of whipped cream.

An unusual compôte can be made from a mixture of strawberries, raspberries and red and white currants, by making a thin syrup of sugar and water and simply pouring it, still boiling, over the prepared fruit. Cherries can be included, but they should be pitted, and cooked briefly in the syrup first. This compôte is best served while still warm or shortly after cooling.

A similar mixture of fruit can be made into an excellent jam. The Swiss make several mixed-fruit jams, including one of raspberries and red currants which is my favorite. From Paris I buy an excellent *confiture des quatres fruits rouges*, as well as concentrated purees of various fruits including strawberry, raspberry and black currant, which provide a quick and easy basis for ice creams and sorbets (water ices).

On the whole, I prefer to leave black currants out of these mixed fruit dishes, for their very strong flavor tends to overpower the other more delicate ones. All alone, however, they make the best of all ice creams, for their acidity cuts through the bland mass of cream. The young leaves of the English black currant bush, used to flavor a thin syrup of lemon juice, sugar and water, make an exquisite sorbet.

Like the black currant, the green gooseberry is best cooked by itself. It is delicious made into a "fool" (by pureeing, and combining with heavy cream and sugar), baked in a tart or pie, or made into an ice cream. An unsweetened puree of gooseberries used to be the traditional accompaniment to mackerel, and I find it good with roast pork as a change from applesauce.

Cultivated blueberries have long been a staple in the United States but are a comparatively recent development in England. They are delicious eaten raw for breakfast, sprinkled with confectioner's sugar. In the United States, they are mixed into batters and made into pancakes, waffles and muffins, and baked in pies. They freeze well, simply packed in plastic bags after washing. The same method works well with currants of all sorts, and with gooseberries.

All about plums

Fresh juicy plums are always a treat, and when cooked their plump flesh and tart flavor bring a sharp sweetness to a rich variety of spicy and unusual dishes

There are some fruits that seem to improve with cooking, and plums are among them. One of the best of all sweet-sour pickles for eating with cold meats and curries can be made from plums. They also make one of my favorite jams, for the plum skin lends a certain substance to the jam which few other fruits can equal. They and game birds are an obvious match, for the plums add their own juicy texture to the occasional dryness of game, and their special tart sweetness to the meat's flavor. I serve a delicious cold sauce of plums to accompany game. Plums also combine well with spices, notably cinnamon and cloves, and in some cases ginger. Cider vinegar complements them, as do honey, brown sugar and orange juice. Anyone with a juice extractor can make delicious fruit juice from ripe plums and this, slightly thickened with cornstarch, makes a version of the Danish dessert *rødgrød*.

For those who like to combine fruit with meat, not added at a late stage (as in the American way of serving glazed ham with pineapple) but integrally, the plum is the ideal choice. There are many North African dishes of chicken and lamb cooked with dried fruit of various kinds, and I find that Russian food extends this range still farther. In the Caucasus, the part of Russia bordered by Turkey and Iran to the south, and by the Black Sea and the Caspian Sea on either side, there grows a sour plum called the *albukhara*, which forms a central part of the regional cooking. It is combined not only with lamb and chicken but also with pork, duck, goose, beef and even fish. In most cases it is used in the form of a sour plum sauce, with the surprising inclusion of garlic, and this sauce is then used either as an accompaniment to cooked dishes, or as an integral part of the dish itself.

I read about Caucasian food after weeks spent experimenting with dishes of meat and fruit, and as so often happens, my reading confirmed what I had already learned. The cooking of that part of Russia demonstrates clearly the only satisfactory way of combining two such intrinsically different elements as meat and fruit, which is by adding a number of other ingredients complementary to both; these act as a bridge between the two flavors. Thus many of these dishes also include chestnuts, quinces, spices and fresh herbs, just as the ever-popular saffron in Morocco helps to blend the *tagines* of lamb and dried apricots, or chicken and prunes. The Russians also make use of dried fruits, and use prunes more or less interchangeably with their sour plums.

The accompaniment to these sorts of dishes is vital, as anyone who has ever tried to serve this sort of fruit dish with potatoes will understand. (Sweet potatoes, on the other hand, make a good combination, especially when cooked with spices.) Although rice seems the obvious choice, there are other grains whose nutty flavor and slight sweetness are even better with these dishes. In Morocco, couscous, and in Russia *bulgur* (cracked wheat) or *kasha* (buckwheat) are the most common choices.

I often put the ingredients for a dish together on the table and study them, for this gives me an indication of what to add and what to take away. When confronted with a lump of raw meat next to a pile of fruit it is hard to comprehend that they are to be merged into one dish, but with the addition of nuts and spices, grains, garlic and yogurt, the whole seems to take on a much more homogenous look.

Like all basically tart fruits, the plum goes well with pastry, whether in the continental fashion of the open tart, or the old English deep-dish fruit pie. Both have something to be said for them; the open tart is prettier, but the pie has the advantage that the pastry does not become saturated with the juice from the fruit, but is merely flavored by the steam.

The Austrians are very fond of plums, and cook them in a variety of ways. One of the most unusual is a hot plum dumpling; each plum is enclosed in dough, poached in boiling water and rolled in crisply fried bread crumbs before serving. These are not easy to make well, for like all dumplings they can be heavy, but when they are successful they are delicious.

Bullaces and sloes are the wild relatives of plums; sloes are really too bitter for anything but making sloe gin, which is a delicious drink and fun and simple to make.

Gaviota plums

Cooking with fruits

Make the most of a delectable crop, and as the days shorten, recall the heat of high summer with the undiminished delights of sun-ripened fruits cooked in pies and puddings

In the early summer, in June and early July, the pleasure of eating the first of the season's fruit is so intense that it seems foolish not to enjoy it in its purest possible form. Home-grown strawberries and raspberries cannot be bettered than when eaten simply with sugar and cream, but as the season wears on, the first joy diminishes, and one is ready to appreciate them in other forms. Strawberries and raspberries make the most delicious desserts: mousses, fools (fruit puree–cream mixtures), ice creams and sorbets. They can also be made into an excellent tart; the secret is not actually to cook the berries but to lay them in a pre-baked pastry case and simply warm them through for seven or eight minutes in a very low oven. The strawberry is at its best in the American shortcake, which should be made with the minimum of sugar; the tart raspberry, on the other hand, is a good foil for the sweetness of meringue, as in a *vacherin*. A most useful sauce can be made with raspberries; their acidity makes a good combination with peaches, while the contrast of colors is most attractive.

Although red and white currants are among my favorites of the soft fruits, both for the sake of their delicate translucent appearance and for their flavor, they are not satisfactory eaten raw owing to their acidity. This applies even more strongly to the black currant; all three are best eaten in cooked dishes.

Dessert gooseberries, those delicious plump and juicy berries of dark red, white and golden yellow, are seldom seen nowadays, even in England. They can be grown in standard form, like rose trees, to make a charming addition both to the garden and to the table. The ordinary green gooseberry is I think best cooked and made into prepared desserts such as pies. Plums too make excellent desserts. Apart from the classic dish in red wine, pears are not very satisfactory

for cooking purposes; their bland taste does not go well with pastry or sponge cake. Apples, on the other hand, are the best of all fruits for cooking; the different varieties are vast, and the crisp flesh of the apple makes a perfect foil for pastry. The cooking apple hardly exists outside England; in France, for instance, a dessert apple is used for the *tarte tartin* and other apple dishes.

The Morello cherry is another example of a good cooking fruit; too acid to eat raw, it can be made into excellent pies, tarts and jams. Its acidity prevents the birds eating it off the trees before it ripens, unlike the sweet cherry.

The combining of fruit and dough into a sweet dessert seems to me a typically English thing. Indeed, the first English settlers in America were so distressed to find no apples with which to make their beloved apple pie that they had apple trees sent out from England. Although in parts of the United States there are fruit desserts with strange names like "apple slump" and "berry grunt," there are many fewer fruit puddings than in England. Most other countries seem to have one or two; in France and Italy one rarely finds more than a pastry tart of apples or sometimes pears. A favorite dish of mine is a Russian one called *les quatres fruits*, a most beautiful dish of translucent glowing red. It is composed of a mixture of four fruits: halved strawberries, pitted red and white cherries and red currants. Simply piled in a glass bowl and sprinkled with granulated sugar, the fruit is left for three or four hours in the refrigerator, during which time it produces its own juice.

Surely the best of all fruit puddings is summer pudding; this supremely English creation can be made with any combination of soft juicy fruits, within a casing of bread. My favorite version is filled with a succulent mixture of raspberries and red currants.

$\mathcal{D}$elicious desserts

Fruit tarts, foamy mousses, refreshing sorbets, snowy, white meringues and homemade ice creams make a cool and tempting finale to a languid summer lunch

It must be years since I ate a dessert in a restaurant, at least from choice and not just to be polite—since the days when I was still at school, and used to be taken out as a treat in the holidays. Being a pastry chef in some restaurants must be sadly unrewarding, for it seems I am not the only one who treats the dessert cart, however appealing to look at, merely as part of the restaurant's visual effect.

Yet a meal for several people in one's own house seems curiously unfinished without some sweet dish to end with, particularly in the summertime, when there are so many delicious fruits available. This is the season for light, frothy dishes, tart with the juice of limes or lemons, unburdened by the weight of starch or the richness of large amounts of cream. As an alternative to whipped cream, I like to make a lighter mixture of cream with equal parts of yogurt and beaten egg white. When served as an accompaniment to acid fruit, such as fresh apricots, it can be slightly sweetened, perhaps with vanilla sugar. The same mixture without sugar, drained overnight in muslin, makes a delicate fresh cream cheese for serving with berries.

Homemade ice creams can be delicious, but when using fruit like strawberries and raspberries which make good purees, I think a "fool," semi-frozen, is as good and is easier to make. In Italy they serve *semi-freddo* desserts. With these very cold dishes, a sweet biscuit is almost obligatory to stop one's teeth aching. They can be bought, but more delicious are the ones made at home. My favorite is the lacy *tuile*, the pretty curved biscuits the French make by rolling them while still warm around a smooth cylinder (French recipes specify a wine bottle while some English ones call for a rolling pin!).

Sorbets, or ices, are more refreshing than ice creams, and fun to make in one's own original flavors. A lemon syrup can be used as the base for making infusions of different flavorings, according to whatever may be growing in the garden. This is the way a black currant leaf ice is made, and an equally delicious sorbet of elder flowers. Each of the different varieties of mint will give its distinctive character to an ice, as will the scented leaves of certain geraniums. Garnished with tiny sprigs of mint, or a few red berries, these pale greenish-white ices look extremely pretty indeed.

All foamy desserts can gain immeasurably from being served in just the right way. Sorbets are particularly suited to tall rather than shallow glasses, since they melt so quickly. At Ballymaloe House, in County Cork, sorbets are served in large bowls molded of ice, which is both attractive and practical. Pretty glass bowls, some in shapes of leaves or flowers, are worth buying if you like to serve this sort of dessert. I remember a lunch given by Maxim's at the Inn on the Park in London at which the dessert was a most delicious raspberry ice cream garnished with strawberries, served in little edible containers shaped ingeniously to look as if folded from squares of cloth. An extravagant gesture—for no one ate the container beyond nibbling at a corner. But it did look charming.

Mousses which have been set with gelatine are best served on a nearly flat plate. At one English country house, fruit mousses and molds used to be served surrounded with little frosted branches of red and white currants, still with the leaves on, the whole sprigs first dipped in beaten egg white and then in powdered sugar. No one could deny that much of the pleasure of eating is visual, especially toward the end of a meal, and details like this vastly increase the diners' enjoyment.

There are two old-fashioned desserts too light to be called puddings, which I particularly like in summer. Both of these are based on a *sauce à la vanille*, the true custard. Caramel meringue is a meringue baked in a caramel-lined mold, then turned out onto a "sea" of custard. The other is *oeufs en neige*, or floating island, a meringue mixture poached in large spoonfuls and served floating in a shallow bowl on the custard sauce. In this one the contrast between the snowy white meringue and creamy yellow sauce makes it one of the prettiest dishes I know. One of my favorite flavorings is caramel, but it is tricky to make: the timing must be very precise, to prevent the liquid caramel forming into hard toffee when it comes in contact with a cooler substance. It also makes a very pretty garnish: you pour a thin layer of caramel into an oiled pan, let it harden, completely, then shatter it into a million tiny golden shards to scatter over the dish.

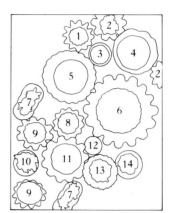

1 *Apple snow*
2 *Mint sorbet*
3 *Orange Boodles fool*
4 *Chocolate apple cream*
5 *Oeufs en neige (floating island)*
6 *Fruit salad*
7 *Nectarine; grape; strawberries; mint*
8 *Sliced nectarines in lime juice*
9 *Raspberry ice cream*
10 *Coeur à la crème*
11 *Blackberry fool*
12 *Caramel mousse*
13 *Strawberries in cream*
14 *Prune whip*

Black currant, blackberry, crabapple, greengage, damson and plum, red currant and quince; the very names of the berries summon up the taste of summer, so simply preserved

1 *Black currants*
2 *Fraises des bois*
3 *Marmalade*
4 *Mint jelly*
5 *Lemon curd*
6 *Four fruit jelly*
7 *Apricot jam*
8 *Red currant jelly*
9 *Raspberries*

It is only recently that I have become addicted to the joys of eating bread and jam—since I started making my own bread. My favorite jams are inevitably those made by myself or my friends, although we do have some excellent commercial jams in England. It is not economical to make your own unless you have fruit from your own garden, but it is nonetheless very rewarding.

Bread and jam is my idea of a delicious snack, especially when combined with a good quality unsalted butter. Some of the most successful jams can be made from quite commonplace fruits, such as an excellent rhubarb and ginger jam, which I make from a friend's recipe. Plum jams, of which greengage and damson are the best, have become favorites in my household.

I like fruit jellies almost better than jam, and they are easier to make, but they are more extravagant. They can be eaten as jam, or as a garnish to meat dishes, or as a glaze for fruit tarts. Crabapple jelly (which I make with fruit from a friend's garden) is good both for eating with bread and as a substitute for red currant jelly, in cooking or for serving at the table with roast lamb, game dishes or baked ham.

Apple and quince jelly is another economical and easily made preserve, with a lovely pinky golden color. Quince jam is delicious with cream cheese. Black currants make a very good jelly, as do blackberries, so long as they are not waterlogged. All the currants are better in jelly than jam, for the tiny pips are irritating if not strained out. The juice of red currants can be advantageously added to other fruits in both jams and jellies, for it lends a tart flavor to sweet berries like strawberries and raspberries, while increasing the pectin content.

I am still very inexperienced at making jams, but I have gathered tips from friends and relatives who have been doing it for years. One is to use preserving sugar rather than any other; it is more expensive but does seem to make better jam. My only piece of advice is to make relatively small amounts at a time, at least until you know you like the finished product, and put it in small jars. A family may get bored before finishing a huge jar, and long to start another while it sits uneaten on the shelf.

Both the Swiss and the French make first-rate jams; perhaps the best—certainly the most expensive—jam in the world is the exquisite white currant jelly made by one French firm, whose tiny octagonal glass jars, filled with a greenish-white jelly with some of the currants suspended in it, have always been to me a symbol of luxury. I found instructions for making this jelly recently in the *Tante Marie Cookery Book*. It involves picking each tiny seed out of every currant with a goose feather, without breaking the skin. The recipe ends with the sound advice, "Do not try to make too much of this at one time." Like all true luxuries, this seems to me a good example of something better bought than made at home.

LES CONFITURES

$\mathcal{P}$ickles and preserves

A larder stocked with jars of neatly labeled chutneys and pickles is the satisfying reward for the traditional housewifely virtues of foresight, economy and industry

The pickling and preserving of food is one of the oldest of culinary arts. Among the Californian Indians, from ancient times, preparations for the winter would be already under way by September. The men would go off on extended hunting trips, while the women spent most of their time collecting acorns and grinding them into flour. This acorn flour formed the staple of their winter diet, either cooked as a mush or baked into bread. When the men returned with slaughtered deer, most of the flesh would be dried for the winter, while many nuts, roots and seeds were put in store. These practices continued with little change from the Stone Age up until the beginning of this century.

In contrast, but different only in degree, was the vast range and amount of food customarily stored for the winter by a northern Michigan farm family of the 1870s. This was probably the most bountiful period in history for the storing of food, since much of the knowledge that had been acquired through centuries was shortly to be rendered almost valueless by technological development in canning, freezing and freeze-drying. Before these developments, the farmer's wife and her helpers would have been occupied for many months, indeed almost continuously throughout the year, in "putting food by." Barrels of flour and dried beans would be stored in the larder, as well as sacks of brown and white sugar, buckwheat and corn flour. Jugs of molasses were collected, and plentiful supplies of coffee, tea and other store-bought staples. In the cellar squash, turnips and cabbages would be heaped, and potatoes and apples stored in bins. Barrels would be filled with cucumbers in brine, and sauerkraut. Jars of preserved fruit would be set in rows on the shelves: cherries, plums, peaches and pears. There would also be giant crocks of pickles, notably mustard pickle, chow chow,

piccalilli and watermelon rind, and crocks of preserved citron, quince, and gingered pears. Bottles of catsup and chili sauce would be accumulated in profusion, since they were much used in conjunction with the staple winter dish of dried beans. Salt pork and pickled pigs' feet would be stored in barrels, and hams hung in the cellar after curing, while high in the attic would be hung strings of peppers and dried apples, nuts and bunches of herbs.

Although the art of pickling is less vital now than in previous centuries, it has lost none of its emotive appeal. Of all the domestic arts, none has more significance, for it acts as a symbol of all the housewifely virtues: foresight, economy and industry. Even from a purely practical point of view, there is a lot to be said for making some preparations for the winter: despite modern technology, we can still find ourselves at the mercy of power cuts, strikes and freak snowstorms when it comes to obtaining and preparing food. Nonetheless, pickling plays a rather different role in our lives nowadays, being used mainly—at least in England—to add variety to our winter diet, and to make use of garden produce at its cheapest and most plentiful.

Strangely enough, the pickles I like best are those preferred by the Michigan farmer: chow chow, piccalilli and mustard pickle. Other favorites of mine are pickled beets and two chutneys: one of mango for serving with curries, the other a mint chutney for eating with crusty French bread and Cheddar cheese.

All in all, making pickles is a very rewarding thing to do, and can earn one much admiration. A great beauty living in New York once said to me, "Men are enormously impressed by beautiful girls making pickles. If you're plain it's not worth the effort; homely girls should find something more exotic to do."

1 *Chow chow*
2 *Pickled eggs*
3 *Pickled onion*
4 *Pickled cucumbers and onions*
5 *Pickled red cabbage*
6 *Mango*
7 *Cranberry relish*
8 *Green tomatoes*
9 *Pickled corn and red peppers*
10 *Mango chutney*
11 *Pickled green beans*
12 *Pickled eggs in beet juice*

cranberry relish p110
chow chow p111
mango chutney p111
pickled red cabbage p112
pickled eggs p112

Fresh from the dairy

Buttermilk, curd cheese, skimmed milk and sour cream, the traditional products of the home dairy, can enhance breads, soups and sauces to great effect

1 *Cream*
2 *Butter being weighed*
3 *Eggs*
4 *Butter churn*
5 *Butter to be shaped*
6 *Parsley butter balls*
7 *Butter in decorative shapes*

In former times almost every British country house had its own dairy (and even the smallest cottage dweller kept a cow, until the abolition of common grazing grounds deprived the cottager of this right in the eighteenth century). The dairy was a pleasant room, cool and quiet, with that strange milky smell which has such strong childhood associations for many of us. It was well ventilated, with a roof of thatch or slate to insulate it against the summer heat. The floor was of stone slabs, the shelves invariably of slate or stone. The windows were slatted to keep out the sun, and the visual effect was a pleasing contrast between the warm golden yellow of butter, milk and cream and the cool grey of slate and stone. There was a feeling of peace and cleanliness. Each day the floor was scoured with fine sand, the containers and implements were scalded with boiling water, rinsed in fresh cold water and left to dry in the open air. Cloths were forbidden and soap was never used. In some of the grander establishments, the ladies of the house made a habit of visiting the dairy to drink milk fresh from the cow and to taste the syllabub; in these cases the dairy was likely to be prettier and less utilitarian, with sprigged china on the shelves. There was usually a separate room for cheese making, opening off the dairy, which was kept for making butter.

After a new law requiring pasteurization was passed in 1933, the home dairy all but disappeared; now children's images of dairy foods are more likely to be of fruity yogurts in bright-colored cartons than of the old butter churn or "Scotch hands," those wooden implements like rectangular ping-pong paddles used for rolling pats of butter. Once a knowledge of this sort goes, it is hard to recreate a feeling for the products it relates to. How many people nowadays can tell the difference between buttermilk and skimmed milk, or curd cheese and cottage cheese? What were curds and whey and what was Miss Muffet doing on that tuffet?

Curds and whey were, of course, a much-loved English dish, often given to children. Without pasteurization, the milk would form naturally into curds; nowadays the separation must be achieved by adding a cheese starter and bacteria to replace those destroyed by sterilizing. The curds were served with some of the slightly sweetened whey poured over them. In Wales, curds were sometimes made from buttermilk and this was less rich. Separating the milk from the cream was done by hand, for cows' milk separates naturally, and after standing for some hours in broad pans, the cream could be easily lifted off with a skimmer. In Devon and Cornwall, where the milk was especially rich, the cream was often clotted before being made into butter.

Butter is made by causing the fat globules in the cream to form into a solid mass. This is done by agitation at a controlled temperature as in churning. There are various types of old wooden churns still to be found; some were operated by a plunger, others by turning the whole churn over and over. One was worked by a dog running over the surface of a large wheel. Once it had formed into a mass, the buttermilk was drained off and the butter was well washed.

It was then kneaded, either by hand or with a wooden roller, and washed again frequently until all the buttermilk had been forced out; if any buttermilk were left in, the butter would soon turn rancid. Packed into barrels and heavily salted, with all the moisture and air driven out, it could be kept for months, then the excess salt washed off before eating. A more practical way of keeping butter is by clarifying it, or turning it into ghee, the cooking fat most used in India. Although it loses its delicious "buttery" taste, it makes an excellent cooking medium which can be kept for long periods.

The three main dairy products—cream, cheese and butter—leave us with a residue of three by-products; skimmed milk, whey and buttermilk. Skimmed milk is made into cottage cheese and is valuable for those on diets, as it contains many of the properties of milk with almost none of its fat. Whey is usually fed to pigs, calves or chickens, although in Italy and some Scandinavian countries it is made into a soft cheese. Buttermilk is the most interesting from the cook's point of view. Fresh buttermilk has a foamy, slightly acid quality. It is the best liquid ingredient for baking scones and soda bread. Sour milk makes a good alternative, but this is also hard to come by, even in Ireland, the home of soda bread. There I was told that the best solution is to make up skimmed milk from powder, and then sour it by adding yogurt or a cheese starter.

*H*igh tea

Somewhere between an afternoon snack and an early supper is the English institution of high tea – simple cooked dishes with bread and butter, tea and cakes

The traditional English tea must be almost a thing of the past. Usually served not in the dining room but rather in a sitting room or the nursery, this informal meal must have been one of the pleasantest aspects of grand country house life. Each house had its own tradition, but the actual dishes served were probably similar. As Lady Sysonby said in her cookbook published in 1935: "The ideal tea table should include some sort of hot buttered toast or scone, one or two sorts of sandwiches, a plate of small light cakes, and our friend the luncheon cake. Add a pot of jam or honey, and a plate of brown and white bread and butter—which I implore my readers not to cut too thin—and every eye will sparkle."

High tea is a compromise between tea and supper. On family holidays in Ireland, we used sometimes to have a high tea for adults and children alike, at about six o'clock. Ireland is the perfect place for informal meals of this sort, for its best foods seem particularly suited to them. The cooked part of a high tea usually consists of eggs, bacon, potatoes, tomatoes, mushrooms or cheese, which when combined with the delicious Irish soda bread and many varieties of "brack," or fruit bread, and marvelous farm butter and fresh milk make an almost perfect meal—not only at tea time, but equally good as a light lunch, supper or breakfast. They are most quickly cooked, usually in a frying pan, and made of ingredients either in the larder or easy to get.

Slices of potato cake with fried eggs and bacon, mushrooms on toast, corned beef hash with poached eggs, bacon with grilled tomatoes; these are ideal dishes for a high tea.

Then the hearty sandwiches: the *croque monsieur* of toasted cheese and ham; the delicious American "BLT"—a bacon, lettuce and tomato sandwich with mayonnaise; or simply toasted bacon sandwiches. And the more elegant sandwiches: watercress or cucumber, potted shrimps on brown bread, cream cheese with guava jelly. A plate piled with buttered toast cannot be improved upon, especially when served with homemade kipper paste. Pancakes of all sorts are a good idea: rolled around pork sausages with a bowl of applesauce alongside; American-style pancakes with maple syrup; bacon pancakes made by crumbling bits of crisply fried bacon into the batter before it's poured onto the griddle; or drop scones, which are really the Scottish pancakes, spread thickly with sweet butter. There is a variety of scones to choose from: plain white ones eaten with butter and jam, cheese scones and fruit scones. A homemade loaf of bread will make any tea table welcoming, especially soda bread, or the potato bread you find in Ireland—so good fried in bacon fat for breakfast. For a cake I generally rely on American brownies to please everyone, because they are easy to make and are so good. I also love "oatjacks" for the same reason; crisp flat cakes made from breakfast oats, these are literally child's play to make. All that is needed beyond this is a huge pot of tea with which to wash down all these good things.

Even writing about these meals makes me feel nostalgic, and I am resolved to bring back the custom of high tea, if only occasionally, during a holiday or over a weekend.

1 *Oatjacks*
2 *Cinnamon toast*
3 *Potato scones*
4 *Brownies*
5 *Marmalade toasts*
6 *Drop scones*
7 *Cheese scones*
8 *Chasse*
9 *Potato pancakes*

When less is best

Shake off the winter's excesses and shape up for summer. Ignore grueling regimens and start to enjoy your diet with light, nutritious, and temptingly presented dishes

1 Radishes
2 Grapes
3 Lentils
4 Chili peppers
5 Bay leaves
6 Mint
7 Rosemary
8 Peppers; cherry tomatoes
9 Capelli d'angelo pasta
10 Marzipan
11 Okra
*12 Wild strawberries; Italian
    parsley; fennel leaves*
13 Cherry tomatoes
14 Brussels sprouts
15 Quails' eggs
16 Cauliflower; rice crackers; rice
17 Cress

The cold windy days of early spring seem an odd time to go on a diet, but it is not so foolish as it seems. We can eat masses of warming and comforting food—dishes like *osso buco*—which may well cheer us up at the time but leave us feeling bloated and overweight, and often consequently depressed, or we can choose to go on a diet; this I recommend in anticipation of the warm weather ahead.

I once spent a few days at a health farm and was greatly impressed by how well I felt on a light diet—in conjunction, I must admit, with lots of fresh air and exercise. As I get older I find I become more and more aware of how I feel, and am just not prepared to put up with feeling less than well. The brain is far more active on a light diet; large amounts of heavy food have a tendency to dull one's awareness.

Although "new" diets are sometimes fun to try out, the more eccentric ones are almost impossible to fit in with normal life, particularly as far as family and friends are concerned. In the long run the best diet is a flexible one based on general principles and one's own tastes. I prefer to concentrate on poached and broiled food, together with lots of raw fruit and vegetables.

During the summer months, light food presents few problems; there is such a wide range of salads and cold dishes, and so much delicious fruit. In the very early spring it is a little more difficult. I favor a number of dishes made from boiled beef, chicken and poached fish, which provide stock for making clear soups and are the basis of a number of hot and cold dishes. One can learn to do without pasta, rice or potatoes, and instead plan to eat a variety of steamed green vegetables, dressed simply with lemon juice. Instead of bread, stock up on a selection of crisp crackers, and use only minute amounts of sunflower seed oil or other light oil for cooking instead of butter or olive oil, and lemon juice instead of vinaigrette. I combine yogurt, mustard, lemon juice and a very little sour cream or low-fat cream cheese to make substitute sauces for mayonnaise and béchamel. Beaten egg white folded into yogurt and very lightly sweetened can take the place of whipped cream, for serving with fruit compôtes. The only alcohol I drink when dieting is white wine with sparkling mineral water, and I attempt to give up coffee, at least in the evenings.

It helps to remember that good habits are just as addictive as bad ones; I know people who have become totally dependent on their daily bicycle riding, swimming or jogging, and the hope is that one can succeed in becoming so attached to one's diet that one chooses to continue with it, at least during the week; then one might eat normal meals at weekends. It is our general eating habits that matter, not the odd meal. In any case, after a few weeks of eating simply, the craving for fattening foods does diminish, and if one is lucky, may cease entirely. Meanwhile, it is more sensible to give in to one's cravings now and then, to eat the cream cake or chocolate bar without undue guilt, or the forbidden image can become a total obsession.

The most important lesson is simply to eat less. This can be made easier in a number of ways: first by buying best quality ingredients in small quantities, which increases our pleasure in eating without costing us much more. Second, we can use smaller plates than usual, and serve soups in small cups instead of bowls. The dishes should be prettily garnished, partly in order to make them look appealing, and partly to camouflage the actual amount of food. We can use garnishes like sliced radish, cucumber and fennel, shredded lettuce and watercress sprigs, foods that are wholesome as well as pretty. It is a good idea to serve the food on individual plates, avoiding the temptation for second helpings. Whenever time permits, and particularly in the evening, serve two or three light dishes instead of just one. A three-course meal takes longer to eat and is more interesting, thus surmounting two of the great problems of dieting.

As an encouragement, I suggest buying a new piece of equipment, something especially relevant to this sort of cooking. If you don't already have one, my first choice would be a pressure cooker; I use this for all "boiled" food, from large pieces of meat to tiny vegetables. (As a rough guide for beginners, divide normal cooking times by three.) And buying a yogurt maker can be economical, since when dieting one tends to use more yogurt as an alternative to cream.

$\mathcal{F}$reezer food

More than simply an extra larder, the freezer can become a treasure chest of good things to be produced with a flourish when time is short, or when a treat is in store

As with most useful inventions, the freezer can be adapted to many different individuals' needs. For someone with a large garden the obvious use is the freezing of garden produce. To me, with a kitchen garden the size of a pocket handkerchief, its other possibilities become apparent. My freezer is in a cottage where I spend weekends and holidays, and I use it in three different ways. First, as a last resort in case I forget to carry even the most immediate essentials from the city; so I always have a loaf of bread and a packet of butter in the freezer, which, together with instant coffee, provides at least a scanty breakfast. Second, I aim to have on hand some first-class basic ingredients for a few main meals: sausages, bacon, a couple of pounds of beefsteak, finely ground and wrapped in half-pound packs, for making hamburgers and Bolognese sauce, a chicken cut in half and wrapped separately for broiling. Usually I have some kipper fillets for making pâté; smoked cod's roe for *taramasalata*; a carton of chicken livers for a smooth pâté; and shrimps or crabmeat for making shellfish cocktails. On a simpler level, frozen fish fillets are always useful for quickly prepared meals.

In the realm of frozen vegetables, I find spinach one of the most useful, both leaf and chopped. It can be used as a base for *oeufs mollets*, for filet of sole, for a green sauce to pour over poached eggs, or for a creamy soup. Frozen corn is also delicious, both on the cob and off; it makes the basis of corn chowders, succotash, egg dishes, fritters and corn puddings. Finally, I like ratatouille, either commercially frozen or homemade, petits pois, whole green beans, broccoli and brussels sprouts.

Yet from my point of view the main advantage of having a freezer is as a sort of extended larder, a storage place for cooked dishes which I make when I have time and eat when I don't. I use it in a relatively short-term way, often cooking a dish one week for the next; and this seems to work well. I am sure that food does deteriorate, in flavor at least, over long periods (although it is still perfectly safe) and I tend to eat most things within a month at the most.

The dishes I make are mostly simple family meals, like pies, pasta, soups. The best ones for freezing are undoubtedly those covered with a lid of some sort, a covering to protect the interior from the inevitable dehydrating effect of the extreme cold. Thus pastry dishes are ideal and the so-called pies covered with a puree of potatoes are also extremely good: both fish pie and shepherd's pie come into this category.

Dishes of pasta are good so long as they are well covered with sauce: noodles, either green or white, in a béchamel sauce flavored with tomato puree and enriched with cream; lasagne, layered with alternate fillings of minced meat and tomato sauce, and covered with a cheese sauce; even a simple macaroni and cheese can be good when made with a creamy and well-flavored sauce.

Pancakes freeze well and are extremely useful; so long as no sugar is added to the batter, they can be used for sweet or savory dishes. They can be frozen plain, or filled with a mixture such as creamed chicken, shellfish or mushrooms.

When tomatoes are plentiful I buy several pounds and reduce them to a thick puree, carefully seasoned and flavored with fresh basil or marjoram. I store the resulting puree in half-pound cartons and use it as a sauce for noodles during the winter. Similarly, when cooking apples are falling off the trees, I make them into a puree and freeze in the same way, to eat with yogurt or cream throughout the winter. Even in my small garden I sometimes have an excess of green vegetables: spinach, sorrel and lettuce. These I make into soups and freeze, adding cream either at this point or when reheating.

At the end of the summer I freeze small bunches of tarragon in plastic bags. This works extremely well and is suitable for basil and marjoram also. *Pesto*, or *pistou*—the Mediterranean paste made from pounded basil, garlic and pine kernels—also freezes excellently; it is the most delicious addition to a minestrone-type soup, or a dish of fettuccine.

Last of all I come to my favorite use of the freezer: as a place to store treats. I find it sad that from the child's point of view the kitchen is no longer the exciting pleasurable place it once was. Few mothers, or aunts or grandmothers for that matter, have the time to make toffee and fudge, cookies and cakes for fun. In the United States most children are allowed to raid the icebox and there is often a giant jar of cookies for general use. In England our more puritan attitude has I am afraid made the kitchen almost out of bounds, at least as far as indiscriminate eating goes. I sympathize with both points of view; on the one hand I like the idea of children being free to help themselves, but I am the first to get annoyed when pounds of fruit vanish in an afternoon. For this reason I think the freezer makes a good compromise: it can be filled with delicious treats —ice cream and sorbets, cookies, waffles and cakes—but it cannot be raided on impulse, since things need time to defrost.

1 *Peppermint ice cream*
2 *Strawberry and raspberry sorbet*
3 *Plum ice cream*
4 *Mocha ice cream*
5 *Oatmeal, chocolate and Catherine wheel cookies*
6 *Crêpes*
7 *Lemon sorbet*

pistou p106
green sauce p107
strawberry and raspberry
  sorbet p113
peppermint ice cream p114
strawberry and raspberry
  ice cream p114
plum ice cream p115

A cookout

Barbecuing is the most primitive of cooking methods, and somehow an excess of equipment and trimmings seems to spoil what is essentially a simple pleasure

1 *Skewered onions*
2 *Skewered tomatoes*
3 *Lobster*
4 *Brochettes of conger eel*
5 *Rosemary brush*
6 *Homemade bread*
7 *Skewered giant prawns*
8 *Clams*
9 *Lemon*
10 *Red mullet in hinged grill*

Barbecue cooking has two aspects, the one as appealing to me as the other is unattractive. Originally it was simply the grilling of raw food, usually meat or fish, over an open fire. Not only does this make an attractive sight, it is also a wholesome method of cooking. Yet in recent years this simplicity has almost been lost under a plethora of modern equipment. The barbecue stoves have become elaborate machines, almost as glossy and alarming as automobiles. With their hoods and rotisserie attachments, they seem to defeat their own purpose, since many of them need electricity, and there is something distinctly unaesthetic in yards of electric cord trailing through the garden.

I am convinced that the nicest barbecues are homemade, whether a permanent feature in a corner of the garden or terrace, or a temporary construction on a beach or at a camping site. One can buy a simple cast-iron grill to be laid on a base built of bricks, and sandwich-shaped wire grills with long handles are also available. These facilitate the turning of such food as hamburgers and small flat fish. Whole fish can, of course, be laid directly on the grill, but turning is sometimes tricky. When barbecuing, care must always be taken to prevent the food becoming burned. If this threatens, the food should be moved slightly farther from the heat than usual, and watched over like a hawk.

Seafoods are my first choice in barbecues; more unusual than meats, they also have the advantage of quick cooking. One can obtain excellent results from barbecuing lobsters, either raw or parboiled. Ideally they should be grilled raw, but this necessitates killing them with a knife, which I cannot bring myself to do. I drop them in boiling water as usual, and boil them only briefly. Lobster tails are also delicious barbecued; simply flatten them, baste with butter and lemon juice, and grill. Giant prawns or shrimps can be threaded on skewers and grilled either in their shells or with only their tails left on for decorative effect. Firm white fish can be cut into cubes, marinated in olive oil and lemon juice, then put on skewers and grilled, occasionally basted with marinade. Clams can be steamed directly on the coals; sprinkle them first with water and wrap them, nine or ten at a time, in foil.

Meat barbecues are more conventional, but delicious nonetheless, and are generally more popular with children. I like to grill a large piece of meat, either a two-inch-thick piece of beefsteak or a whole leg of lamb, boned and slightly flattened, in one piece, and then cut it in strips before serving. On the scene a heavy chopping board and a sharp knife are essential. Pork and lamb chops to be grilled should be trimmed of excess fat to prevent flare-ups. Sausages, particularly frankfurters, are always popular with children. Spareribs are best grilled in whole racks, basted with a sweet and sour sauce, then cut in ribs to be eaten by hand. I like tender lamb cut in cubes and marinated, then threaded on skewers and grilled over dried twigs of rosemary, and served with hot flat bread. Barbecued chicken drumsticks are easily eaten in the fingers, but I prefer small chickens cut in half, flattened, marinated and then grilled, with a teriyaki sauce for basting.

Sauces and marinades play an important part in barbecue cookery, since the fierce heat might dry out the meat if it is not basted. The only foods I prefer without sauce are steaks, hamburgers, sausages and boned leg of lamb. In other cases I find the best sauce is dictated by the character of the food itself. Shellfish—and other fish—are best basted with melted butter and lemon juice, though the butter must be replaced with oil if the fish needs marinating. Small pieces of lamb, like chops or skewering cubes, are best basted with a mixture of olive oil and lemon, with chopped onion and added herbs. Pork, being a fat meat, needs little oil but is excellent in a sweet mixture of soy sauce and brown sugar or honey. Thin sauces can be applied with a bulb-type baster while thicker ones need a brush. I like to make my own brush from a small bunch of rosemary twigs tied together.

Vegetables can also be barbecued quite successfully. Small onions, whole tomatoes or parboiled beets can be threaded on skewers and basted with butter while grilling. Corn fresh from the garden can be roasted on the cob over charcoal or in foil placed among the coals. The latter method is also good for potatoes: a medium-size potato will take about three-quarters of an hour to become well cooked.

The pleasures of the picnic

The open air whets the appetite and sharpens the senses, so eschew the sandwich in favor of outdoor food planned with imagination and served with flair

I find cooking for picnics a very rewarding task. For one thing it is a versatile meal with scope for a wide choice of dishes; also I find that people are less critical, more appreciative in fact than usual, and with better appetites. For a change the food is not the sole focal point; the weather, the view, the general surroundings are all as important. The main thing is to have fun, and since guests are likely to be of all ages, I like to make the food as widely varied as possible.

One way of providing a large choice but with some unity is to concentrate on one or two sauces and serve a large number of different foods to eat with them. My fondness for Middle Eastern foods stands me in good stead here, since many such dishes make ideal picnic food. A variation on a Lebanese sauce is easily made by mixing equal parts of *tahini* (a sesame seed paste not unlike peanut butter in consistency), yogurt and lemon juice. Other good sauces can be made by combining cream cheese or buttermilk with garlic and fresh herbs in a blender. These smooth thick sauces are easy to transport, and they go well with a variety of good picnic foods, like roasted chicken pieces, meatballs, tiny fried fish cakes, hard-boiled eggs, sausages, crudités of all sorts, potato chips, small whole tomatoes, crisp leaves of romaine lettuce, and new potatoes, boiled or baked in their skins. Flat pita bread, heated in the oven and wrapped in foil just before setting out makes the ideal accompaniment to these foods, most of which appeal to children.

An excellent Middle Eastern *meze*, or hors d'oeuvre, is a spread made of pureed eggplant and tomatoes with olive oil and lemon juice. Packed in a carton and carried to the picnic site to be spread on small squares of rye bread or pumpernickel, this makes a delicious appetizer. Another good picnic food is stuffed eggs. I find these so fragile to pack that I carry the yolk mixture separately, and only fill the whites at the last moment, at the picnic.

As an alternative to meatballs, I sometimes make a flat meat loaf of ground lamb under a thick tomato sauce; this hardens on cooling and can be cut in slices and eaten with the fingers. For a dessert I recommend making a baking pan full of chocolate brownies and transporting them in the pan, covered with foil. An alternative idea is a rich fruit cake and wedges of hard cheese— Gruyère, Cheddar or Emmenthal. Apples, bananas and grapes are the best fruit for picnics, since they are easy to pack and to eat.

A totally different sort of picnic that occurs more frequently in my life is the evening picnic, almost always for a small group of grownups only. Here it seems worthwhile to be more extravagant. I like to construct this sort of picnic as if it were a formal meal, by serving it on china plates with proper silver and glassware on a pretty tablecloth spread on the grass. Several bottles of chilled white wine, or even better, champagne, are almost obligatory. To start, perhaps homemade potted shrimps with small sandwiches of brown bread and butter, or some shellfish with mayonnaise. Then possibly small chicken pies, served warm; or a roll of flaky pastry enclosing a large spicy sausage served with mustard sauce; or a quiche, served warm, made with spinach and tomatoes or mushrooms. A different menu might be hot *consommé madrilène* or borsch, served in small cups, and followed by a cold main dish such as smoked chicken or turkey, cold duck, or a game pâté, with crusty French bread and a green salad. Slices of cold rare roast sirloin are good for picnics rolled around freshly grated horseradish.

During hot weather, a totally cold meal might be a first course of smoked fish of some sort— smoked trout skinned and filleted for easy eating, or slices of smoked salmon rolled around a mousse of smoked mackerel—followed by a *chaudfroid* of chicken and a dish of mixed vegetables in a light vinaigrette. For the dessert, I might make individual coffee mousses in *oeufs-en-cocotte* dishes, or a wine gelatine; or I might simply take some of the most elegant chocolate truffles I could find in my favorite shop.

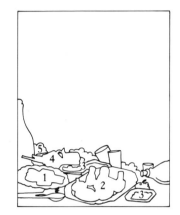

1 *Stuffed cucumbers*
2 *Chaudfroid of chicken*
3 *Borsch en gelée*
4 *Salad of lettuce, scallions, fennel*
5 *Grapes*

$\mathcal{S}$tocking up

Some foods take kindly to canning, some keep best when dried or pickled; the judiciously stocked larder means meals to be proud of at all times of the year

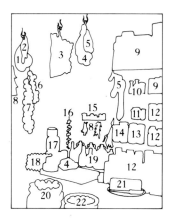

1 *York ham*
2 *Pepperoni sausage*
3 *Side of bacon*
4 *Hams*
5 *Salamis*
6 *Garlic*
7 *String of onions*
8 *Dried herbs*
9 *Dry staples*
10 *Liquid staples*
11 *Mustard*
12 *Canned goods*
13 *Olive and sunflower seed oils*
14 *Bottled fruits*
15 *Homemade preserves*
16 *Dried wild mushrooms*
17 *Cheeses*
18 *Eggs*
19 *Homemade wine*
20 *Potatoes*
21 *Veal and ham pie*
22 *Pickled eggs*

clam chowder p66
celery hearts mornay p100
tomato and pepper
  sauce p103

Over the years, the British larder has changed its character. Originally a cool room on the north-facing side of the house, with shelves of slate and netted windows, it was intended as a storage place for food that could be kept over a period of time: for hams and sides of bacon, root vegetables in sacks, and eggs pickled in brine or waterglass. It was at its fullest in the autumn, when it would be stocked to capacity with food to last through the winter. In America too, most houses had larders well into the twentieth century, but vegetables such as potatoes, onions, cabbages, turnips and squash were customarily placed for storage in a pit dug in the ground and then covered over, while parsnips were left to freeze in the soil where they grew, until needed.

At that time, the preserving of food by various methods had been going on for hundreds of years, and had become a highly developed skill. After the invention of the tin can in 1812—bottling had been developed by a Frenchman a few years earlier—many of these skills fell into disuse and were forgotten. Elaborate methods of keeping food had been a necessity, not just for the average household which had some fresh food to fall back on during the winter, but for ships on the long sea voyages to America and India. When the Mayflower landed off Cape Cod in 1620, its 100 passengers had been living for three months on a diet of hard tack, dried fish, cheese and beer. Two hundred years later, however, the preserving of food had become a much more finely developed art, and some live animals were usually taken on board to be killed during the trip. A woman traveling to India in 1850 took with her, for her own consumption, squares of soup concentrate made by boiling down chicken legs with veal bones until thick and gelatinized; salted duck potted with herbs; condensed cream; fresh lemons; sprouted watercress to be grown in the cabin; and "kitted" chickens—an ingenious sort of vacuum pack of suet paste for preserving whole chickens.

Nowadays, just as canning and freezing have supplanted the old ways, so the larder has been superseded by storage cupboards, at least in urban areas. The original feeling of the passing year has been lost, for tin cans know no season.

I find the most successful canned foods fall into three categories. First, the fish products: tuna fish, sardines, anchovy fillets, cod's roe and minced clams are all delicious and unfailingly useful. Second, the vegetables: Italian plum tomatoes, condensed tomato paste, and sweet red peppers; haricots, flageolets, and red kidney beans; chick peas and petits pois—unlike fresh peas but good nonetheless; sweet corn, celery hearts, and endives; red cabbage and sauerkraut to combine with fresh or tinned frankfurters for a sustaining meal. Last, the juices: my favorite is the mixed vegetable juice which the Americans export; it is excellent drunk alone with ice or as a substitute for tomato juice in a Bloody Mary; heated as a soup; mixed with yogurt or sour cream as a sauce; or used as an ingredient in cooked dishes such as navarin of lamb. Straight tomato juice from a can is also good, as is clam juice, which can be served chilled as an appetizer with a squeeze of lemon juice, heated as a consommé, or used as the base for a delicious fish sauce. There is a good tinned clam chowder, but you can make a better one from a can of minced clams, some bacon, potatoes and milk. Jellied consommé or *consommé madrilène* is useful; it can be served chilled as a cold soup or used as a substitute for aspic in cold dishes. One can buy tinned Greek *dolma*, but much better results are obtained by simply buying the vine leaves, in cans or from a Greek shop in brine, and making the stuffing with fresh ingredients. Canned *tortillas* are good for serving with *guacamole* and other cold vegetable dishes made with oil. Prune juice survives bottling or canning well, and that most popular American chocolate syrup, available in cans, is always welcomed by children, particularly when poured over vanilla ice cream.

When stocking up my larder in the country for a definite period of time, like the summer holidays, I think almost the most important things to have are the minor things, the spices and flavorings which I have come to rely on for so many dishes, but which can be hard to find in country shops. I usually make a special shopping trip before leaving to stock up on things like risotto rice, saffron, dried mushrooms, good French mustard, feta cheese packaged in brine, mozzarella for pizza, pine nuts, plenty of good olive oil, white wine vinegar, French or Belgian cooking chocolate and a whole Italian salami.

No larder is complete without at least a few homemade foods: jars of jams or sauces, bottled fruits, even a few dried herbs from the garden, or wild mushrooms strung on a knotted string and hung in a warm place to dry.

64

Summer recipes

The number of people each recipe serves is indicated wherever appropriate.

shellfish soup

2½ cups shellfish such as mussels or clams,
or scallops
2 leeks
1 stalk celery
2 potatoes
3 tablespoons butter
2½ cups milk and cream, mixed (half-and-half)
pinch of powdered saffron, or 2 tablespoons finely
chopped parsley
black pepper

SERVES 4–5

Scrub the shellfish (except the scallops) well
and put them still in their shells into a heavy
pan with 1¼ cups water. Bring to the boil,
lower heat and cook for a few minutes,
uncovered, until they open. With a slotted
spoon take out each one as it opens; remove
from their shells and keep warm. If scallops
are included, these will need to be removed
from their shells and then poached gently in
the shellfish stock for 3–4 minutes, before
being lifted out and kept warm. Strain the
stock and reserve. Wash the leeks well and
slice finely. Chop the celery and peel and
thinly slice the potatoes. Melt the butter in a
heavy saucepan and sauté the leeks. Add the
celery and potatoes, and 1¼ cups hot water.
Bring to the boil, lower the heat, and simmer
for about 25 minutes with the lid partially
covering the pan, until the vegetables are
soft. Heat the half-and-half until almost
boiling and add. Reheat the fish stock, adding
the saffron (if used), and stir into the soup. At
this stage the soup may be put into a blender
for a smoother texture; I prefer the coarser
version, however, which is more like a
chowder. Cut the large shellfish in pieces and
add all to the soup. Keep just below
simmering point for 4–5 minutes, until all is
well heated, and serve.

clam chowder

3 oz bacon
4 tablespoons (½ stick) butter
1 large onion
2 potatoes
one 7 oz can minced clams
1 tablespoon flour
2½ cups milk
2 tablespoons chopped parsley
pepper

SERVES 4–5

Chop the bacon in small pieces and fry slowly
until crisp. Chop the onion and add 2
tablespoons butter and the chopped onion to
the pan. Fry gently until the onion is golden,
stirring frequently. Peel and dice the potatoes
and add to the pan; pour on enough hot water
to barely cover them. Bring to the boil, reduce
heat and simmer for 15–20 minutes, until the
potatoes are soft. Add the minced clams and
their juice, bring back to the boil, reduce
heat, and simmer another 2–3 minutes. Mix
the flour and a little of the milk to a paste; add
to the pan, and stir until smooth. Bring the
rest of the milk almost to the boil, and
immediately pour into the clam mixture. Stir
in the remaining butter, add plenty of black
pepper, sprinkle the chopped parsley on top,
and serve as soon as possible.

beet and fennel soup

½ lb beets
3¾ cups chicken stock
1 lb fennel
4 tablespoons sour cream
salt and pepper

SERVES 5–6

Peel the beets and chop them finely by hand
or in a food processor. Put them in a heavy
pan, add the stock and bring to the boil.

Reduce the heat and simmer gently for 30 minutes. Meanwhile chop the fennel finely. Add to the soup and simmer for another 30 minutes, covered. Add water or stock during cooking if it seems too thick. Cool slightly. Put into the blender and blend briefly. Return to the pan, stir in the sour cream gently and adjust the seasoning.

jellied borsch

2 lb beets
½ Spanish onion
4 envelopes (1 oz) gelatine
2½ cups chicken stock
2–3 tablespoons lemon juice
salt

SERVES 6–8

The day before: scrub the beets, peel and chop in a food processor, or by hand. Put into a pressure cooker with 3½ cups very lightly salted water. Bring to the boil and cook for 30 minutes under 15 pounds pressure. Cool and remove the cover according to manufacturer's directions. Strain and measure the stock; you should have about 2½ cups. Discard the beets. Slice the onion finely and add to the beet stock; refrigerate overnight. Strain again. Melt the gelatine in the chicken stock, and add to the beet stock. Add lemon juice to taste. If there are any lumps, strain the mixture. Refrigerate until set. To serve, roughly chop the aspic and spoon into cups.

jellied consommé

1 large piece knuckle of veal (about ¾ lb)
2–3 lb beef bones
½ lb shin of beef
1 onion
½ lb carrots
½ lb turnips
4 stalks celery
1 lb tomatoes
4 stalks parsley
1 bay leaf
½ lb beets
1 lemon
salt and pepper

SERVES 8–10

Put the meats and bones into a large pot. Cover with about 4 quarts water, and bring to the boil extremely slowly. It should take about 45 minutes to boil. Skim off the scum as it rises to the surface. Meanwhile chop the onion, carrots, turnips and celery. Peel and cut up the tomatoes, discarding the seeds. When the stock is boiling, and clear, add the chopped vegetables and the parsley and bay leaf. Bring back to the boil, reduce heat and simmer for 6 hours, covered. Pour through a strainer or colander lined with a double layer of cheesecloth. When it is cool, put in the refrigerator and leave overnight, or for several hours, long enough to solidify the fat. Remove the solid fat from the surface and discard. Taste the soup; if the flavor is weak, or if the consommé is not firm enough to form a gelatine, bring to the boil and simmer for about 15 minutes, to reduce and strengthen it. Peel and chop the raw beets, and drop into 2 cups boiling salted water. After 20 minutes strain off the juice, and add to the soup, to color it. Add salt, pepper and lemon juice to taste. Strain again; allow to cool and finally chill before serving. Besides being served as a jellied consommé, this can be used as an aspic, perhaps turned out of a ring mold and filled with shellfish or lobster meat, or from individual molds filled with lightly cooked vegetables such as green peas. And it can of course be served as a hot clear soup.

Soups/chicken and vegetable

soupe au pistou

1 *onion*
2 *small leeks*
2 *small carrots*
2 *zucchini squash*
6 oz *green beans*
¾ lb *tomatoes*
½ lb *shelled fresh, or* ¼ lb *dried haricot beans*
2 oz *elbow macaroni*
2 oz *basil leaves*
2 *cloves garlic, chopped*
4 *tablespoons pine nuts, chopped*
2 oz *grated Parmesan cheese*
½–¾ *cup olive oil*
SERVES 8

Chop the onion, leeks and carrots. Cut the zucchini in ½-inch slices and the green beans in 1-inch pieces. Peel the tomatoes, discard the seeds and chop them coarsely. Heat 2 tablespoons olive oil in a broad heavy pan and sauté the onion and leeks gently until pale golden. Add the carrots and haricot beans, and 5 cups hot water. Bring to the boil, add salt, and simmer 45 minutes. (If they are dried, the haricot beans should be precooked for 30 minutes.) Add the zucchini, green beans and tomatoes to the soup and simmer for another 30 minutes. Add the macaroni, and cook another 12–15 minutes until tender. Meanwhile prepare the pistou: chop the basil leaves and pound them in a mortar. Add the chopped garlic and the chopped nuts. Pound all together into a smooth paste, then add the grated cheese. Continue to pound until smooth and blended; then beat in the remaining oil very gradually, pounding all the time, until you have obtained a creamy paste like thick butter. Put the paste in the bottom of a heated soup tureen and add the boiling soup gradually. Mix well and place in a barely warm oven 5–10 minutes before serving.

tarragon soup

This recipe is equally good with dill or chervil in place of tarragon

2 *tablespoons fresh tarragon, chopped,*
plus 3 sprigs left whole
2 *tablespoons butter*
2 *tablespoons flour*
3¾ *cups hot chicken stock*
1 *egg yolk*
1 *tablespoon lemon juice*
salt and pepper
SERVES 3–4

In a large heavy pan, melt the butter, stir in the flour and cook for 1 minute. Add the hot stock and stir until blended. Simmer gently for 3 minutes. Add the sprigs of tarragon, and salt and pepper, and turn off the heat. Cover the pan and leave for 30 minutes. Taste, and if the flavor seems faint, reheat until almost simmering, and turn off again. Strain into a clean pan and reheat until almost boiling. Beat the yolk of egg with lemon juice in a small mixing bowl. Stir in one ladleful of the hot soup, mix and pour back into the pan. Stir over a very low heat for about one minute. Add the chopped tarragon and serve.

crème Sénégal

This is a most delicious and unusual soup, which can be served hot or cold. If preferred, the chicken meat may be omitted

2 *tablespoons butter*
1½ *teaspoons light curry powder*
2 *tablespoons flour*
3¾ *cups strong chicken stock*
juice of ½ *lemon*
⅝ *cup cream*
¼ lb *breast of chicken, chopped*
salt and pepper
SERVES 4–5

Melt the butter in a saucepan over a medium heat and stir in the curry powder and then the flour. Cook gently for 3 minutes, stirring often. Heat the stock and add, a little at a time, stirring as it thickens. After 3–4 minutes, add the lemon juice, the cream and salt and pepper to taste. If you wish to serve this as a hot soup, the chopped white meat should be added at this stage and heated gently before serving. For a cold soup, cool the pan quickly in a container half-full of ice-cold water, stirring now and then to prevent a skin forming. When cool, refrigerate for 2–3 hours, and add the chopped chicken to the soup just before serving.

chicken noodle soup

bones of 1 chicken
3 small carrots
¼ lb green beans
2 small leeks
2 small zucchini squash
2 small tomatoes
½ cup star noodles, or rice
2 tablespoons chopped fresh herb—tarragon, chervil, basil or dill
salt and pepper
SERVES 3–4

Put the chicken bones in 1 quart salted water and bring to the boil; reduce the heat, and simmer for 1 hour. Strain the stock and remove the bones after salvaging any scraps of meat clinging to them; return these pieces of chicken to the stock. Cut the carrots, beans, leeks and zucchini in ½-inch slices. Peel and quarter the tomatoes, discarding the seeds. Bring 2 cups lightly salted water to the boil and add the carrots. After 5 minutes, add the beans, then the leeks, the zucchini and the tomatoes, at 5-minute intervals, in that order.

Meanwhile reheat the chicken stock. When the vegetables are tender, lift them out with a slotted spoon and transfer them to the chicken stock. Drop the noodles or rice into the vegetable water, bring to the boil, lower the heat and simmer until tender. Drain, and add them to the soup. Season with salt and pepper to taste and stir in the chopped herb. Stand for 5 minutes before serving. Have a bowl of Parmesan on the table.

kitchen garden soup

1 bunch watercress
1 cucumber
2 potatoes
½ head lettuce
3 tablespoons butter
3¾ cups hot chicken stock
⅝ cup cream
salt and pepper
SERVES 5–6

Chop the watercress coarsely, stalks and all. Peel the cucumber, cut in half lengthwise, discard the seeds and chop. Peel the potatoes and slice them fairly thickly. Shred the lettuce. Melt the butter in a heavy pan and add all the vegetables. Sauté gently for 5–8 minutes. Add the stock, bring to the boil, lower the heat and simmer, covered, for 30 minutes, adding salt and pepper to taste. Mash the vegetables roughly with a fork, and adjust the seasoning. Add the cream, stir in over low heat until heated through, and serve.

gazpacho

Everyone has a favorite recipe for gazpacho; this is the one I usually make. It can be made more quickly in a blender, but I prefer this version, in which each ingredient is chopped separately. A food processor can be used to accelerate the process for chopping everything except the tomatoes (for these are reduced to pulp too quickly in a processor)

1 *cucumber*

1 *lb tomatoes*

1 *Spanish onion*

1 *green pepper*

2 *cloves garlic*

2 *slices dry whole wheat bread*

1¼ *cups mixed vegetable juice or tomato juice*

1¼ *cups chicken stock*

4 *tablespoons olive oil*

2 *tablespoons wine vinegar*

salt and pepper

SERVES 6–8

Peel the cucumber and skin the tomatoes, chop, and remove the seeds. Finely chop the onion and green pepper and put them with the cucumber and tomatoes into a large bowl. Mince the garlic and add. Remove the crusts from the bread, cut it in small dice, and stir into the mixture. Add the tomato or vegetable juice, the chicken stock and oil and vinegar, and salt and pepper to taste. Chill in the refrigerator for several hours or overnight. About 1 hour before serving, add 6–8 ice cubes and taste for seasoning. If necessary, thin the soup with ice water, or more stock.

zucchini soup

2 *lb zucchini squash*

1 *medium-size onion*

4 *tablespoons (½ stick) butter*

1 *medium-size potato*

4½ *cups chicken stock*

4 *tablespoons heavy whipping cream*

3 *tablespoons chopped basil (if available)*

salt and pepper

SERVES 6–8

Chop the onion. Melt the butter in a heavy pan and sauté the chopped onion until pale golden. Cut the zucchini in chunks and add to the pan. Cook gently for about 8 minutes, stirring often. Peel and slice the potato, and add to the pan. Gradually add the stock, stirring, and salt and pepper; cover the pan and simmer for 25 minutes. Cool slightly, then pour into a blender, and puree. Reheat, adding more salt and pepper if required. Stir in the cream, and sprinkle with the chopped basil (if available). Let stand for a few minutes before serving.

snow pea soup

This soup is also extremely good if chilled before serving

½ *lb potatoes*

3¾ *cups chicken stock*

1 *small onion*

½ *lb snow peas*

3 *tablespoons butter*

pinch of sugar

⅝ *cup cream*

salt and pepper

SERVES 6

Peel the potatoes, slice and put in a pan with the stock. Bring to the boil, reduce heat, and simmer for about 20 minutes, until soft. Meanwhile chop the onion finely; cut the ends off the peas, and cut each pod in two or three pieces. Melt the butter in a sauté pan, and add the onion and then the peas. Cook gently for 5 minutes, stirring occasionally. Add to the potatoes, bring back to simmering point, and cook gently for another 5 minutes, not longer or the peas will spoil. Cool slightly, and press through a sieve. Reheat the puree gently, adding the cream, sugar and seasonings.

lima bean soup

1 lb lima beans, frozen or fresh
2½ cups chicken stock
1¼ cups milk
⅝ cup cream
2 tablespoons very finely chopped lean ham
salt and pepper
SERVES 6

Cook the beans in the stock until soft. Heat the milk and cream together. Put the beans in a blender with the stock and add the milk and cream. Blend. Pour into a clean pan, add salt and pepper to taste, and reheat gently. Serve at once, with a little chopped ham on top of each bowl of soup.

cold watercress soup

1 bunch watercress
3 tablespoons butter
2 cups hot chicken or beef stock
2½ cups buttermilk
SERVES 4

Wash and chop the watercress, stalks and all. Melt the butter in a saucepan and add the watercress; sauté gently, stirring occasionally, for about 8 minutes. Pour in the stock. Simmer for 20 minutes, then cool. Stir in the buttermilk. Pour the mixture into a blender and blend. Chill before serving.

sorrel soup

¼ lb sorrel
¼ lb watercress
4 tablespoons (½ stick) butter
1 medium-size potato
3 cups hot chicken stock
1¼ cups buttermilk
SERVES 4–5

Chop the sorrel and the watercress and stew them gently in the butter in a heavy pan for about 5 minutes. Peel and slice the potato. Add to the pan and stir in the stock. Cover and simmer for 35 minutes or until the potato is soft. Cool slightly, then pour into the blender. Blend well and then pour into a bowl. Stir in the buttermilk. Chill before serving. For a hot soup, substitute a half-and-half mixture of milk and cream for the buttermilk, and reheat gently before serving.

cold cucumber soup

2 large cucumbers
2 cups chicken stock
2 cups buttermilk
2 tablespoons chopped fresh mint, or a dash of Tabasco
salt and pepper
SERVES 6

Peel the cucumber and cut in chunks, discarding the seeds. Put the stock, which must be free from all fat, into the blender with the buttermilk. When blended, add the cucumber. Blend again until it is in tiny pieces, but not yet entirely smooth. Add salt and pepper to taste. Chill for 2–3 hours before serving, then garnish each bowl with chopped fresh mint, or stir in a dash of Tabasco.

tomato and cucumber soup

I love this soup, which has a very light fresh taste; it is like a gazpacho but more subtle

1 lb tomatoes
2 cucumbers
1 bunch scallions
2 tablespoons butter
3¾ cups hot chicken stock
4 tablespoons sour cream
juice of ½ lemon
salt and pepper

SERVES 4–5

Peel and cut up the cucumbers, discarding the seeds. Slice the scallions in thin slices. Melt the butter in a heavy pan and sauté both gently for 5 minutes. Add the hot stock, and simmer for 20 minutes. Pour into a blender and blend briefly. Return to the clean pan and add the sour cream, lemon juice, salt and pepper. Peel the tomatoes, discarding the seeds, and chop them finely; stir into the soup. Add the sour cream and serve either hot or cold. If cold: chill well before serving. If hot: heat only once (gently) after adding the sour cream, just before serving.

carrot and tomato soup

This is a totally raw soup, to be served cold

1 lb carrots
1 lb tomatoes
juice of 1 small orange
⅝ cup yogurt

SERVES 3–4

Peel the carrots and tomatoes and cut them in chunks, discarding the tomato seeds. Put into a blender, with the orange juice. Blend until smooth, and stir in the yogurt. Serve immediately.

tomato soup

This is a hot soup but is also very good chilled

1½ lb ripe tomatoes
2½ cups chicken stock
1 teaspoon sugar
1 tablespoon lemon juice
2 tablespoons chopped herb—basil, chervil or dill
salt and pepper

SERVES 4–5

Peel the tomatoes and cut in quarters. Heat the stock in a large pan and, when it is nearly boiling, drop in the tomatoes. Add salt, pepper and sugar, and bring back to the boil; simmer for 5 minutes, then remove from the heat. Press through a medium-mesh sieve and return to the pan. Reheat, adding the lemon juice and more salt and pepper if needed. Serve in cups, sprinkled with chopped herb.

cold lentil soup

An unusual cold soup that is quite substantial without being heavy

1⅓ cups lentils
1 lb frozen chopped spinach
2½ cups buttermilk
juice of 1 lemon

SERVES 6

Cover the lentils with plenty of cold, lightly salted water. Bring slowly to the boil, lower the heat and simmer, covered, until soft, about 45 minutes. Drain. Meanwhile, cook the spinach briefly, not more than 1 minute, and drain; put it into the blender with the buttermilk. Blend well, and pour into a bowl. Stir in the whole lentils. Add lemon juice to taste, and chill.

Eggs/first and main course dishes

eggs with watercress puree

6 eggs
2 bunches watercress
2½ cups hot chicken stock
3 tablespoons butter
2 tablespoons flour
⅝ cup cream
2 tablespoons grated Parmesan cheese
salt and pepper
SERVES 6

Wash the watercress and chop it coarsely, stalks and all. Cook in about 2 cups of the stock, just simmering, for 5 minutes. Pour into a blender and blend to a puree. Melt 2 tablespoons of the butter and add 1 tablespoon flour; stir over medium heat. Add the watercress puree and stir well until mixed. Simmer for a few moments, then add 1 tablespoon cream. Season with salt and pepper, and set aside to keep warm. Cook the eggs in boiling water for 5 minutes exactly; cool them under running water just enough so they can be shelled. Put them into a shallow dish and keep warm. Melt the remaining butter and add the rest of the flour; cook briefly, stirring, then add the remaining stock and stir until thickened and smooth. Cook gently for 2–3 minutes, then add the rest of the cream and stir in the grated cheese. Stir until melted and add salt and pepper to taste. Pour the hot watercress puree over and around the eggs and dribble the sauce over the top.

eggs with purslane

5 eggs
1 bunch purslane
3 tablespoons butter
salt and pepper
SERVES 2

Use only the tender part of the purslane, probably the top two inches of the stalk. Wash and dry well in a towel, and chop. Melt the butter in a frying pan and add the purslane. Cook briskly, until wilted, 3–4 minutes. Meanwhile beat the eggs, and season them with salt and pepper. Pour into the pan on top of the purslane. Cook like an omelette but without trying to fold it over. Serve immediately on a warm platter.

oeufs à l'estragon

4 eggs
⅝ cup heavy whipping cream
3–4 sprigs tarragon
salt and pepper
SERVES 4

Preheat the oven to 325°F. In a saucepan, heat the cream until nearly boiling. Add the sprigs of tarragon, reserving four nice leaves for garnish. Cover the pan and set aside for about 15 minutes in a warm place. Break the eggs into buttered cocotte dishes, add salt and pepper and put in the oven. After about 8 minutes, when the eggs are almost set, pour the hot cream through a strainer, dividing it between the 4 eggs. Lay a tarragon leaf on top of each, return to the oven for 2 more minutes, and serve at once.

Eggs/first and main course dishes

eggs and potatoes with yogurt

4 eggs
2 lb potatoes
2 tablespoons butter
⅝ cup yogurt
¼ lb shelled peas (or ½ lb in pods)
salt and pepper
SERVES 4

Peel and boil the potatoes and drain well; mash them with butter, and plenty of salt and pepper. Cook the peas in boiling salted water until just tender. Lift them out with a slotted spoon and add them to the potatoes with the yogurt, stirring to mix thoroughly. Poach the eggs in lightly simmering salted water; drain. Spoon the potato into heated bowls, and put a poached egg into each. Serve immediately.

eggs in green peppers

4 eggs
4 green peppers
3 tablespoons butter
1 medium-size onion
⅝ cup rice
salt and pepper
SERVES 4

Cook the rice in plenty of boiling salted water until just tender; drain well. Preheat the oven to 350°F. Drop the peppers into a large pan of boiling water and cook for 20 minutes. Lift out carefully, drain and cool slightly. Cut off the tops, scoop out the seeds and discard. Chop the onion. Melt the butter and sauté the onion until golden. Add the rice and mix well, and add salt and pepper to taste. Spoon into the green peppers, and make certain they will stand upright. Break an egg into each. Sprinkle the top with salt and pepper and bake for 12 minutes. Serve with fresh tomato sauce 1 (see recipe, page 103).

eggs with sausage and peppers

4 eggs
1 onion
1 green pepper
2 tablespoons butter
1 clove garlic
1 chili pepper or a dash Tabasco
one 12 oz can tomatoes, roughly chopped
one 6 oz can red peppers, drained and chopped
pinch of sugar
2 kabanos (or other spicy sausage)
salt and pepper
SERVES 4

Chop the onion and green pepper, keeping them separated. Melt the butter in a heavy pan and sauté the onion gently. Crush the garlic and add with the green pepper. Finely mince the chili pepper (if used) and add it or the Tabasco, and the tomatoes and red peppers. Simmer gently for 30 minutes, covered, stirring occasionally. Add salt and pepper and a pinch of sugar. Cut the sausage in thin slices and add for the last 5 minutes of cooking. Fry the eggs and spoon the pepper mixture onto a dish and lay the eggs on top.

stuffed eggs

6 eggs
2 tablespoons sour cream
4 tablespoons chopped herbs:
tarragon, chervil, dill, chives
salt and pepper
SERVES 4–6

Boil the eggs for 12 minutes, cool them quickly under cold water and shell. Cut them in half lengthwise. Scoop out the yolks into a bowl; mash to a paste with a fork, adding the sour cream and salt and pepper to taste. Fold in the chopped herbs. Spoon the mixture into the halved egg whites just before serving.

egg croquettes

7 *eggs*
1 *small onion*
4 *tablespoons (½ stick) butter*
1¼ *cups milk*
½ *bay leaf*
pinch of mace or nutmeg
4 *tablespoons flour*
2 *tablespoons chopped parsley or ham*
1 *cup dry bread crumbs*

SERVES 3–4

Hard boil 6 eggs; let cool, shell and chop finely. Chop the onion. Melt 2 tablespoons of the butter and gently sauté the onion. Heat the milk with the bay leaf and mace or nutmeg, but not to boiling point. When the onion is soft and lightly colored, stir in 2 tablespoons of flour and add the warm milk (after removing the bay leaf). Mix well. Add the chopped eggs and parsley or ham and mix again; season to taste with salt and pepper, and pour into a lightly greased shallow dish. Cool, then cover and refrigerate several hours or overnight. The next day shape the mixture into oval (egglike) shapes; roll each one first in flour, then dip into beaten egg, then into dry bread crumbs. Fry in the remaining 2 tablespoons of butter, turning on all sides, until heated through and browned. Serve with tomato sauce 1 (see recipe, page 103).

eggs with potatoes and leeks

4 *eggs*
1½ *lb potatoes*
1 *lb leeks*
4 *tablespoons (½ stick) butter*
1¼ *cups milk*
salt and pepper

SERVES 4

Peel the potatoes and boil in salted water until tender; drain well. Meanwhile, wash the leeks well and chop them coarsely. Melt the butter in a frying pan and add the leeks. Cook gently for 8–10 minutes. Heat the milk, and pour about half of it over the leeks. Cover the pan and cook for another 10 minutes or until the leeks are soft. Mash the potatoes with the remaining milk, and stir in the leeks, with their juices. Add enough of the remaining milk to make a fairly thin puree. Season to taste with salt and pepper. Keep hot while you poach the eggs. Pour the potato-leek mixture into 4 warmed bowls and place a poached egg in the center of each.

baked eggs with cheese

6 *eggs*
6 *slices bread*
6 *oz Cheddar, Gruyère or Emmenthal cheese*
2 *tablespoons butter*
salt and pepper

SERVES 3–6

Preheat oven to 400°F. Cut the crusts off the bread. Butter the bottom of a baking pan just large enough for the six slices to be laid flat, close together. Cut the cheese in thin slices and lay them on the bread. Break the eggs over the cheese; sprinkle with salt and pepper. Bake for 15 minutes or until the whites have just set. Cut in pieces and serve with a green salad.

Eggs/quiches

herb quiche

2 cups flour

3 oz grated Cheddar cheese

6 tablespoons (¾ stick) butter

1 egg yolk

¼ lb spinach

¼ lb sorrel leaves

1 bunch watercress

5 or 6 scallions

2–3 tablespoons chopped parsley

1 tablespoon each chopped tarragon, chervil and dill weed

2 eggs

½ lb Demisel or Carré cheese

⅝ cup heavy whipping cream

salt and pepper

SERVES 4–8

Preheat oven to 400°F. In a mixing bowl mix the grated cheese, flour and a pinch of salt with your fingertips; cut the butter in with a pastry blender. Sprinkle the mixture with 4 tablespoons of very cold water. Blend lightly; add more water if necessary to unite the ingredients. Chill for 30 minutes before using. Roll out and line a 10-inch pie plate or quiche pan. Prick with a fork in several places. Brush with beaten egg yolk and bake for 10 minutes. Reduce heat to 350°F. Remove from the oven. Wash the spinach, sorrel, watercress and scallions and drop into boiling salted water. After 4 minutes, drain well, squeeze out all moisture, and chop, with the herbs. Beat the eggs, mix with the cream and Demisel or Carré cheese, and add salt and pepper to taste. Stir in the greens and mix lightly. Pour the mixture into the pastry shell and return to the oven. Bake for 30 minutes, or until set and browned on top.

spinach and cheese quiche

This quiche is best eaten hot, but it is also quite good cold for a picnic

½ lb pastry (see recipe, page 126)

2 eggs + 1 yolk

1½ lb fresh spinach

1 tablespoon butter

¼ lb ricotta or cream cheese

⅝ cup cream

4 tablespoons grated Parmesan cheese

salt and pepper

SERVES 4–5

Make the pastry, and line a 9-inch quiche pan with it. Chill. Preheat oven to 375°F. Wash and chop the spinach. Beat the yolk. Brush the cold pastry with beaten egg yolk, prick with a fork and bake for 10 minutes. Wash and chop the spinach; put it in a saucepan with the butter and cook gently until soft. Drain well, squeezing out as much moisture as possible. Add salt and pepper to taste, and spoon into the prebaked pastry shell. Beat the remaining two eggs and add the ricotta or cream cheese, gradually, as you beat. When the mixture is smooth, stir in the cream, and add most of the grated Parmesan. Stir well and pour over the spinach. Scatter the reserved Parmesan evenly over the top, and bake the whole quiche for a further 30 minutes at the same temperature, or until it is set and nicely browned.

shellfish salad

1 lb any firm white fish
½ bay leaf
1 tablespoon vinegar
6 scallops
6 crawfish or lobster tails (cooked)
½ lb prawns or shrimp (cooked)
juice of 3 lemons
1 head iceberg lettuce
1 large green pepper
1 cucumber
4 hard-boiled eggs
6 tablespoons olive oil
1 cup mayonnaise (see recipe, page 104)
salt, pepper and peppercorns

SERVES 6

Add enough water to the fish just to cover. Add ½ bay leaf, the vinegar and a few peppercorns. Poach the fish gently until it can be flaked with a fork but remains firm, about 10–12 minutes, and leave to cool. Remove the skin and bones and break in large flakes. Pour the juice of 1 lemon over the fish flakes and leave for about 30 minutes. Poach the scallops for 5 minutes in the same court bouillon; cool, then marinate in lemon juice the same way. Shell the lobster or crawfish tails and shrimps or prawns, and soak for 10 minutes in a bowl of very cold salted water. Drain thoroughly. Wash the lettuce, break up the leaves in neat pieces and shake to dry. Cut the pepper in strips and the peeled cucumber in sticks. Put the lettuce into a large salad bowl and cover with the pepper and cucumber. Pile the white fish in the center, and arrange the shellfish over the top. Surround with the halved hard-boiled eggs and pour over the salad a vinaigrette made by mixing together 6 tablespoons olive oil and 2 tablespoons lemon juice, salt and pepper. Mix the salad at the table, and hand the mayonnaise around.

chicken salad

one 2½–3 lb chicken
1 head crisp lettuce
1 cucumber
1 large green pepper
1 head fennel
1 bunch watercress
2 stalks celery
5 or 6 scallions
4 tablespoons lemon juice
3–4 tablespoons sunflower seed oil, or other light oil
salt and pepper
herb sauce (see recipe, page 105)

SERVES 6

Place the chicken in boiling salted water to cover and poach gently for 60 minutes; leave to cool in its stock. Remove from the liquid and cut the chicken meat in pieces, removing skin and bones. Sprinkle the chicken pieces with 3 tablespoons lemon juice. Shred the lettuce. Peel the cucumber and cut in chunks. Slice the pepper and the fennel. Chop the watercress, reserving the best leaves. Slice the celery and reserve any leaves. Slice the scallions. Mix all together and dress with the oil and remaining lemon juice, and seasoning to taste. Serve with the herb sauce, using the reserved leaves for its garnish.

Salads/leaf vegetables

oriental salad

1 *bunch radishes*
1 *bunch scallions*
1 *head chicory or curly endive*
1 *tablespoon lemon juice*
3 *tablespoons sunflower seed oil, or other light oil*
pinch of sugar
black pepper
SERVES 4

Start the day before. Cut the leaves off the radishes, leaving a short, fresh-looking piece of green stem on each radish. Trim off "tails" by cutting a thin slice off the bottom of each radish. Using a small sharp knife, cut a line from the "tail" end to just below the stem. Make 8–12 such cuts on each. With the point of the knife, separate each pair of cuts from the body of the radish to form a "flower petal" attached at the stem end. Cut away both ends of the scallions, leaving only the white and a short length of green. Cut several long vertical gashes at both ends, leaving the middle section intact. Put the radishes and scallions in a bowl of cold water and refrigerate for several hours or overnight. The next day, the cut parts will have curled back into fantastic flowerlike shapes. Drain and pat dry with paper towels. Remove the green outer leaves of the chicory and use the pale inner part only. Separate it into small lacy leaves; wash and pat dry. Put in a shallow bowl or dish with the radishes and scallions in the center. Mix the oil, lemon juice, sugar, and pepper, and sprinkle all over the dish just before serving.

mixed salad

1 *lb tomatoes*
½ *Spanish onion*
1 *bunch watercress*
juice of 1 lemon
pepper
SERVES 4

Peel the tomatoes and cut them in slices. Slice the onion finely. Put the tomatoes into a salad bowl and scatter the sliced onion over them. Add the tender sprigs of watercress, discarding the tough parts, and toss with the tomato and onion. Sprinkle with freshly ground black pepper and the lemon juice. Toss well and serve.

avocado, tomato and mozzarella salad

This is best served alone as a salad course rather than as an accompaniment to other main dishes

2 *avocados*
1 *lb tomatoes*
1 *lb mozzarella cheese*
juice of ½ lemon
6 *tablespoons olive oil*
2 *tablespoons white wine vinegar*
1 *teaspoon oregano*
salt and pepper
SERVES 6–8

Peel the avocados, halve them to remove the seeds, and cut them in slices. Squeeze the lemon juice over them to prevent discoloring. Skin and slice the tomatoes, and cut the mozzarella in slices. Arrange the three ingredients in a bowl and sprinkle them with salt and pepper. Mix the oil and vinegar and pour this dressing evenly over the salad. Sprinkle the oregano over all, and serve.

garden-thinnings salad

This delicate salad is best served with very mild simple foods such as scrambled eggs or omelettes, or poached fish

about 4 *handfuls of young leaves of lettuce, sorrel, spinach, rocket, dandelion, mustard or similar greens*

½ tablespoon lemon juice

2 tablespoons sunflower seed oil, or other light oil

pinch of sugar

freshly ground black pepper

SERVES 4

Wash the leaves well and pat dry with paper towels. Pile them in a salad bowl and sprinkle the sugar over them, and a few turns of the peppermill. Mix the lemon juice and the oil, and add. Toss lightly and serve.

watercress and orange salad

This is particularly good with cold game or roast duck

2 bunches watercress

3 small oranges

2 tablespoons chopped shallots

1 tablespoon lemon juice

1 tablespoon orange juice

4 tablespoons olive oil

salt and pepper

SERVES 4

Pinch the tender sprigs from the watercress, wash and shake dry. Put into a salad bowl. Peel the oranges with a sharp knife, removing all the pith. Divide them carefully in sections and mix with the watercress. Scatter the chopped shallot over all. Mix the lemon and orange juice, olive oil, and salt and pepper. Pour over the salad and toss well.

bacon and dandelion salad

This salad is best as a separate course, either as an hors d'oeuvre, or after a light main course. It is also very good made with young spinach leaves or sorrel, or even a mixture of the two

2 bunches dandelion leaves (about 6oz)

¼ lb bacon

2 slices dry white bread

2 tablespoons butter

1 clove garlic

3 tablespoons olive oil

1 tablespoon white wine vinegar

salt and pepper

SERVES 4

Wash the dandelion leaves and pat dry between paper towels. Cut them across in slices and pile them lightly in a salad bowl. Cut the bacon in small pieces and fry slowly until very crisp; drain and cool. Remove the crusts from the bread and cut the bread in cubes. Add the butter to the remaining bacon fat in the frying pan, and fry the cubes of bread, with the peeled clove of garlic, stirring them around until evenly colored a light golden brown. Mix together the olive oil and vinegar and add salt and pepper; pour this dressing over the leaves. Toss well. Discard the garlic clove and scatter the croutons and the bacon pieces over the leaves and mix lightly. Serve as soon as possible.

fennel and tomato salad

This Italian salad makes a good hors d'oeuvre

2–3 *heads fennel*
1 *lb ripe tomatoes*
2 *tablespoons olive oil*
½ *tablespoon lemon juice*
½ *tablespoon white wine vinegar*
salt and pepper

SERVES 3–4

Wash the fennel and cut across in thin slices, reserving the leaves. Put the slices into a bowl of cold water in the refrigerator for an hour or two to become crisp. Drain and dry well between paper towels. Peel and slice the tomatoes. Arrange the fennel and tomato slices around a platter. Sprinkle salt and pepper over them. Mix the oil, lemon juice and vinegar well and spoon over the vegetables. Chop the reserved leaves of fennel and scatter over the top.

spinach, bacon and mushroom salad

½ *lb spinach*
½ *lb small mushrooms*
juice of ½ lemon
4 *slices bacon*
2 *slices dry bread*
1 *tablespoon butter*
1 *clove garlic*
6 *tablespoons olive oil*
2 *tablespoons white wine vinegar or lemon juice*
salt and pepper

SERVES 4

Wash the spinach and drain well. Discard the stalks and cut the leaves across in thin strips. Wipe the mushrooms, remove the stalks and slice the caps. Squeeze the lemon juice over them. Fry the bacon slowly until crisp, drain on paper towels and break in small pieces. Remove the crusts and cut the bread in small cubes. Peel the garlic clove, and add it, with the butter, and fry the croutons until golden brown. Toss all together in a bowl after discarding the garlic. Add salt and pepper to taste, and dress with the oil and vinegar or lemon juice. Toss well.

pita salad

1 *cucumber*
1 *lb tomatoes*
1 *green pepper*
1 *piece pita bread*
¼ *lb feta cheese*
6 *tablespoons olive oil*
3 *tablespoons lemon juice*
salt and pepper

SERVES 4

Peel the cucumber and cut it in strips like thick matchsticks. Peel the tomatoes, slice them thickly, and cut in similar strips, discarding seeds and juice. Cut the pepper in strips likewise. Toast the pita briefly. (It can be cut in half and put in an electric toaster.) Cool; then tear in pieces. Mix all together in a bowl and season with salt and pepper. Chop the cheese roughly and scatter over the salad. Dress with oil and lemon juice.

orange and almond salad

Like all salads with orange, this is excellent with cold duck, goose or game

1 *head romaine lettuce*

1 *bunch watercress (optional)*

2 *medium-size oranges*

1 *oz flaked almonds*

1 *tablespoon chopped shallot*

1 *tablespoon orange juice*

3 *tablespoons lemon juice*

3 *tablespoons olive oil or peanut oil*

pinch of sugar

salt and pepper

SERVES 4–5

Cut the lettuce across in 1-inch pieces. Cut the stems from the watercress and separate into sprigs. Put with the lettuce in a salad bowl. Peel the oranges carefully, removing all pith; cut them in half lengthwise, and then in slices across, saving any juice. Lay the orange half-moon slices over the green salad, and scatter the flaked almonds over them. Mix the fruit juices, shallots, oil, salt and pepper. Pour over the salad and toss well.

pine nut salad

This pretty salad—green and pink and white—is delicious with cheese

1 *cucumber*

1 *heart of crisp lettuce*

1 *green eating apple*

1 *bunch watercress*

1 *bunch radishes*

4 *tablespoons pine nuts*

3 *tablespoons sunflower seed oil, or other light oil*

1 *tablespoon lemon juice*

salt and pepper

SERVES 4

Peel the cucumber, discard the seeds, and cut it in small dice. Peel and core the apple. Chop the lettuce heart, the apple and the watercress, stalks and all. Slice the radishes finely and mix all together in a large bowl. Scatter in the nuts and season with salt and pepper to taste. Dress lightly with the oil and lemon juice mixed together.

potato and vegetable salad

1 *head crisp lettuce*

½ *lb new potatoes*

3 *or 4 new carrots*

¼ *lb shelled peas*

1 *small cauliflower*

½ *lb small tomatoes*

5 *or 6 scallions*

4 *hard-boiled eggs*

4 *tablespoons olive oil*

2 *tablespoons white wine vinegar*

4 *tablespoons cream*

3 *tablespoons chopped chervil*

salt and pepper

SERVES 4

Wash the lettuce. Cook the unpeeled potatoes and the carrots, peas and cauliflower separately until just tender; leave to cool. Before they are completely cooled, peel the potatoes and slice them thickly. Mix them with the other cooked vegetables in a bowl and pour half the oil and vinegar over them. Put the lettuce leaves in the salad bowl; add the peeled tomatoes, left whole if they are small, or quartered if larger, and the scallions, white part only. Add the cooked vegetables and the remaining oil and vinegar. Season with salt and pepper and mix lightly, without breaking the ingredients. Pour on the cream and mix again. Shell the eggs, cut them in half, and lay them around the edge of the bowl. Scatter the chopped chervil generously all over the salad, and serve.

broiled trout

4 *trout*
4 *tablespoons (½ stick) butter*
1 *tablespoon lemon juice*
salt and pepper
SERVES 4

Preheat the broiler. Make two or three small diagonal cuts on both sides of each fish; sprinkle with salt and pepper. Heat the butter with the lemon juice until melted. Lay the fish in a pan and cook under the broiler, basting with butter and lemon juice. Cook for about 5 minutes on each side close to the flame (about 2 inches away), then for 4–5 minutes farther away (4–6 inches). Continue basting as necessary. To serve, lay the fish on a platter, pour the pan juices over them, and garnish with lemon wedges. Serve with boiled or steamed potatoes.

baked trout with cucumber

6 *trout*
4 *tablespoons (½ stick) butter*
juice of 1 lemon
few sprigs fresh tarragon, chervil or dill, or
1 *tablespoon finely chopped parsley*
1 *medium-size cucumber*
1¼ *cups cream*
1 *tablespoon finely chopped parsley, tarragon, chervil or dill*
SERVES 6

Preheat oven to 375°F. Have the trout cleaned but with their heads and tails left on. Lay them in a well-buttered ovenproof dish and pour the lemon juice over them. Add salt and pepper and the fresh sprigs of herbs. Cover the dish with a buttered piece of aluminum foil and bake for 10 minutes. Meanwhile, peel the cucumber and cut in sticks like thick matchsticks. Melt about 2 tablespoons butter and sauté the cucumber sticks for 2–3 minutes, stirring. Add the cream and bring to the boil while stirring to mix with the cucumber sticks. Remove the fish from the oven and uncover. Pour the cucumber-cream mixture over the trout. Cover and return them to the oven for a further 5 minutes, then remove the sprigs of herbs. Serve garnished with the chopped fresh herbs, and accompany with boiled or steamed potatoes and a green salad.

trout fillets in oatmeal

4 *trout*
½ *cup milk*
5 *tablespoons coarse oatmeal*
4 *tablespoons (½ stick) butter*
1 *lemon*
salt and pepper
SERVES 4

Cut off the heads and tails of the fish; lift each side carefully from the central bone, leaving the skin on. Dip the fillets in milk, sprinkle with salt and pepper, and roll in oatmeal. Fry them in butter, or alternatively put under the broiler dotted with the butter cut in small pieces. In either case, turn the fish carefully, trying to avoid knocking off the oatmeal. When nicely browned on both sides, serve with wedges of lemon. A mustard sauce (see recipe, page 106) also goes well with this.

trout en gelée

4 *trout*

1 *onion*

1 *carrot*

1 *stalk celery*

1 *bay leaf*

3 *stalks parsley*

2 *or 3 cloves*

1¼ *cups dry white wine*

2 *teaspoons coarse salt and 6 black peppercorns*

SERVES 4

A day in advance, make the court bouillon. Stick the cloves in the onion. Put the onion, carrot, celery, bay leaf, parsley, salt and peppercorns into a pan with the wine and 2½ cups water. Bring to the boil, lower the heat, cover, and simmer for 25 minutes. Meanwhile clean the trout but leave the heads and tails on. Add to the simmering court bouillon, and poach very gently for 7–8 minutes, until the trout are cooked. Lift them out carefully; cut off the heads and tails and remove the skin, and put heads, tails and skins back into the pan. Lay the fish on a shallow dish. Boil up the stock to reduce it until you have about 1¼ cups of liquid. Strain and cool. Cut the cooked carrot in thin slices and lay three or four on each fish. Pour about a third of the cooled fish stock over them and chill. When it has set, repeat the process twice. When the third layer has been added, refrigerate overnight. The following day, either serve in the same dish or cut out each fish from its surrounding aspic, lay on a platter and surround with the rest of the aspic cut in small cubes. It is delicious when served with curry sauce (see recipe, page 107).

poached rainbow trout

4 *rainbow trout*

1 *onion, stuck with 3 cloves*

1 *carrot*

1 *stalk celery*

1 *leek*

3 *stalks parsley*

1 *bay leaf*

1 *small bundle fresh herbs: lovage, burnet, tarragon, chervil and dill*

⅝ *cup dry white wine or vermouth, or*

4 *tablespoons white wine vinegar*

1 *tablespoon coarse salt*

10 *black peppercorns*

SERVES 4

Cut the onion, carrot, celery and leek in large pieces and put them into a large heavy pan. Add the bay leaf, fresh herbs, salt, peppercorns and the wine vinegar. Add enough cold water to cover the fish, and bring to the boil. Reduce the heat and simmer, covered, for 20–30 minutes. Lower the trout into the simmering court bouillon; bring back to the boil and then adjust the heat so that it barely simmers. Poach the fish for 7–8 minutes, until just cooked. Lift out carefully and drain. It is delicious when served with shallot sauce (see recipe, page 105) or easy hollandaise sauce (see recipe, page 108).

baked stuffed carp

one 2–2½ lb golden carp
1 oz buckwheat
1 small onion
5 tablespoons (⅝ stick) butter
3 tablespoons chopped parsley
2 shallots
4 tablespoons sour cream
4 tablespoons lemon juice
SERVES 4

Heat ¼ cup very lightly salted water until boiling. Put in the buckwheat and bring back to the boil. Boil hard for 1 minute, then lower the heat as much as possible, cover the pan, and leave to simmer very slowly for 10–12 minutes, until all the water is absorbed. Do not stir. Leave to cool. Chop the onion and cook in 2 tablespoons butter until golden. Stir in the cooked buckwheat and mix well. Add salt and pepper to taste, stir in the chopped parsley, and allow to cool before using. Preheat oven to 350°F. Fill the carp with buckwheat stuffing. Thickly butter the bottom of an ovenproof dish. Chop the shallots very finely and scatter over the butter. Lay the fish on the shallots and sprinkle with salt and pepper. Dot the remaining butter in small pieces over the surface of the fish. Lay a piece of foil over the fish and bake for 40 minutes. Mix the sour cream and lemon juice, and pour over the fish. Put back in the oven, without the foil, and bake for another 10 minutes, or until the fish flakes easily when pierced with a fork. Scatter with chopped parsley, and serve as soon as possible.

anguilles au vert

2 lb small freshwater eels, skinned and cut in 2-inch chunks
4 shallots
3 tablespoons olive oil
½ lb mixed sorrel, spinach and watercress
1 cup celery leaves
2 tablespoons chopped parsley
1 tablespoon chopped chervil
1 tablespoon chopped tarragon
1¼ cups fish stock
1¼ cups dry white wine
1 bay leaf
salt and pepper
SERVES 4–5

Chop the shallots and cook gently in the oil in a heavy pan until soft. Wash and chop all the green leaves except the bay leaf, and add to the shallots. Cook slowly for about 10 minutes, stirring often. Add the pieces of eel and enough fish stock mixed with an equal amount of white wine to barely cover the eel. (If too much is used the sauce will not set to a jelly.) Add the bay leaf, salt and pepper and cover the pan. Bring to the boil and boil hard for 1 minute. Reduce the heat to the lowest possible and simmer for 20 minutes. Remove the bay leaf and serve immediately, in shallow soup bowls. Accompany with a dish of boiled potatoes. Alternatively, it can be served as a cold dish. Leave to cool, then refrigerate overnight; the liquid will set to a thick green aspic. Serve with brown bread and butter.

goujons of sole

2 *Dover or other sole, filleted*
2 *egg yolks*
2 *tablespoons olive oil*
¾ *cup dry bread crumbs*
1 *tablespoon peanut oil*
SERVES 3–4

Skin the fillets and cut them in diagonal strips, about ¾ inch wide. Pat dry with paper towels. Beat the egg yolks with the olive oil and 2 tablespoons water. Dip each fish piece in this mixture, then in dry bread crumbs. Shake off any excess. Heat the peanut oil in a sauté pan until very hot but not smoking. (A small cube of bread should sizzle immediately on being dropped in.) Cook the goujons quickly, turning on all sides until golden brown, for not more than 3 minutes. Drain briefly on paper towels and serve with tomato sauce 2 (see recipe, page 103), horseradish sauce (see recipe, page 107) or simply with quarters of lemon.

sole with watercress sauce

4 *large fillets of sole (and their bones)*
1 *onion*
1 *carrot*
1 *stalk celery*
1 *bay leaf*
3 *stalks parsley*
2 *tablespoons white wine vinegar*
4 *tablespoons medium-fat cream cheese*
4 *heaping tablespoons chopped watercress leaves*
salt, pepper and peppercorns
SERVES 4

Cut the onion, carrot and celery in large pieces and put into a pressure cooker with the fish bones. Add the bay leaf, parsley, salt and 6 peppercorns. Add 3¾ cups of cold water and the vinegar. Bring to the boil and cook for 15 minutes under 15lb pressure. Reduce the pressure according to the manufacturer's directions, and remove the lid when safe. Cool slightly, then put in the fillets and poach gently (not under pressure) for 5 minutes. Lift the fillets out and lay them on a serving platter; keep warm. Strain 1¼ cups of the cooking liquid and put into a blender with the cream cheese and the watercress leaves. Blend, then pour into a small pan and reheat, adding salt and pepper as needed. Pour some over the fillets and serve the rest separately in a small pitcher.

baked cod

2½–3 *lb cod or haddock*
juice of 2 lemons
½ *cup (1 stick) butter*
3–4 *tablespoons dry bread crumbs*
salt and pepper
SERVES 4–6

Preheat oven to 350°F. Place the fish in an ovenproof dish and pour the lemon juice over it. Dot with the butter, and add salt and pepper. Cover with a buttered piece of aluminum foil and put in the oven to bake for about ½ hour. Take the dish from the oven, remove the foil and skin the top side of the fish. Baste with pan juices, then cover with a thick layer of bread crumbs. Return to the oven and bake another ½ hour, basting two or three times more.

Fish/sea fish and shellfish

fish in aspic

3 fillets any white fish
1 carrot
1 onion
1 stalk celery
1 bay leaf
2 tablespoons white wine or white wine vinegar
¼ lb frozen petits pois
2 tomatoes
1 or 2 sprigs fresh tarragon
2 tablespoons lemon juice
1 envelope (¼ oz) powdered gelatine
salt and 6 black peppercorns
SERVES 3

Skin the fillets and cut each one in half. Put the skins into a pan with the carrot, onion, celery, bay leaf, salt and peppercorns. Cover with cold water and add the wine or wine vinegar. Bring to the boil and simmer for 30 minutes. Cook the peas briefly in a little boiling salted water; drain and cool. Skin the tomatoes and chop finely, discarding seeds and juice. Strain the fish stock and bring back to the boil. Roll the fillets and drop them into the stock. Add a sprig of tarragon after reserving six good leaves for garnish. Poach very gently for about 5 minutes, then lift out the fish and drain. Taste the stock, and if it seems weak, boil for a few minutes to reduce it. Strain it again and measure out 1¼ cups. Flavor with lemon juice. Dissolve the gelatine in 1 tablespoon water and stir into the measured stock. Strain again and pour a thin layer into each of six *oeufs en gelée* molds, or any standard-size gelatine molds. Put into the refrigerator to set. When firm, lay one leaf in each mold, then a rolled fish fillet and finally the peas and tomatoes. Cover with the rest of the fish stock gelatine mixture and return to the refrigerator to set. Serve with a light curry sauce (see recipe, page 107).

smoked haddock with eggs

2 medium-size smoked haddock (finnan haddie)
4 eggs
1¼ cups milk
1½ tablespoons butter
2 tablespoons flour
⅝ cup cream
1 tablespoon finely chopped parsley
pepper
SERVES 4

Cut the fish in large pieces, and put them into a shallow pan. Pour the milk over them, and enough water to barely cover the fish. Bring to the boil, cover the pan and remove from the heat. Leave for 15 minutes. Lift out the fish and strain the stock. Boil this until sufficiently reduced and well flavored. Take care it does not get too salty. When cool, flake the fish, removing all skin and bone. Put into a serving dish and keep warm. Melt the butter, blend in the flour, add ⅝ cup reduced fish stock and the cream. Stir over a low heat for 3 minutes, seasoning to taste with pepper. Meanwhile, poach the eggs in salted boiling water. Pour the sauce over the eggs and sprinkle with parsley.

barbecued lobster

2 medium-size lobsters or 4 lobster tails
lemon butter (see recipe, page 105)
SERVES 4

Drop the lobsters into boiling salted water; after 10 minutes, lift them out and cool slightly. Cut each in half with a sharp knife and lay them, shell side down, on the barbecue grill. Cook them for 5 minutes, basting the exposed flesh side with the sauce. Turn over and grill for another 5 minutes. For lobster tails, bend them backward to break the spring of the tail shell and allow 6 minutes' grilling on each side.

potted shrimps

2 lb tiny cooked shrimp in the shell, or
¾ lb shelled cooked shrimp
½–1 cup (1–2 sticks) butter
½ bay leaf
pinch of ground mace
coarsely ground black pepper

SERVES 4

Cut the butter in pieces and melt it in the top of a double boiler, or in a large bowl standing over a saucepan of simmering water. Add the bay leaf and mace and leave for 5 minutes. Add the shrimps and some freshly ground black pepper. Stir gently, then cook for 10 minutes, stirring now and again. Spoon the shrimps into a china dish that holds roughly 2 cups. Add enough butter mixture to come level with the shrimps but not cover them completely. Cool, then refrigerate for 24 hours. In this form they should be eaten within two days. Alternatively, cover the shrimps completely with a second layer of melted seasoned butter, in which case they will keep for two weeks, although you will lose the fresh, juicy flavor. (They can even be stored in the freezer for up to two months, but in this case they will taste no better than the commercially produced variety.) Serve with small sandwiches of thin brown bread and butter, or freshly made toast.

barbecued shrimps

1½ lb large shrimp, uncooked
lemon butter (see recipe, page 105)

SERVES 4

Either leave the shrimps in their shells, or peel them leaving the tails on. Thread them on four skewers, and grill slowly over charcoal, basting continuously with the sauce, for about 4 minutes on each side.

curried shellfish

¾ lb (weight without shells) cooked shellfish such as scallops, crabs, lobster tails, shrimp
3 tablespoons butter
2 onions
2 cloves garlic
½ teaspoon ground turmeric
½ teaspoon ground coriander
½ teaspoon ground cumin
¼ teaspoon ground chili peppers
2 tablespoons ground almonds
2½ cups fish, chicken or vegetable stock
juice of 1 lime or ½ lemon
1 tablespoon red currant jelly
4 tablespoons shredded coconut
salt and pepper

SERVES 4

If you do not have stock, make it by simmering the shells of the shellfish in lightly salted water. Put half the stock aside, with the coconut soaking in it, for 30 minutes. If the shellfish include scallops the scallops should be poached gently for 4 minutes in slightly salted water and drained. Chop the onions. Melt the butter in a heavy pan and sauté the onions until pale golden. Crush the garlic and add to the pan. Stir in the four ground spices and cook gently another 4 minutes. Add the ground almonds and cook another 2–3 minutes. Pour on half the heated stock. Warm the jelly and press it through a sieve. Add it with the lime (or lemon) juice to the pan. Strain the coconut from the stock and put the liquid into the pan; stir well to blend. Taste for seasoning, adding salt and pepper or more spices as required. Add the shellfish to the pan. Heat all together gently; pour into a serving dish. Serve with rice.

Poultry/chicken

casserole-roasted chicken

one 3–4 lb chicken
4 tablespoons (½ stick) butter
juice of 1 lemon
sprigs of fresh herbs: marjoram, tarragon, chervil,
dill, thyme, basil

Preheat oven to 300°F. Heat the butter in a
heavy casserole and brown the chicken all
over. Pour the lemon juice over the chicken
and add the herbs, still on their stalks. Cover
and bake for 1½ hours, turning the chicken
occasionally. To serve, throw away the herbs,
carve the bird and pour the pan juices over it.
Good with rice, noodles, or boiled potatoes
and a green salad.

chicken with grapes

one 3–4 lb chicken
6 tablespoons (¾ stick) butter
juice of 1 lemon
juice of ½ orange
3–4 shallots
½ lb grapes, mixed black and white
SERVES 4

Preheat the oven to 300°F. Heat gently
4 tablespoons of butter in a heavy casserole
and brown the chicken all over. Pour the
lemon and orange juices over the chicken.
Cover and bake for 1½ hours. Meanwhile
chop the shallots and sauté in the remaining
butter until browned. Add the unpeeled
grapes to the sauté pan and cook gently for
5 minutes, stirring now and then until they
are hot and coated with fat. Serve the chicken
on a platter surrounded by the grapes and
shallots, with the pan juices in a sauce boat.

broiled chicken on skewers

one 4–4½ lb roasting chicken, cut in pieces
4 tablespoons (½ stick) butter
juice of 1 lemon
2 cloves of garlic, finely chopped
SERVES 4

Cut the uncooked chicken off the bones,
remove all skin and cut in neat pieces. (Save
the bones and scraps for soup.) Thread the
chicken pieces on skewers and broil. Melt the
butter, add the lemon juice and garlic; baste
the chicken with this mixture frequently for
12–14 minutes, as the meat is lean and has no
skin to protect it. Serve on a bed of rice with
the basting juices poured over. Accompany
with avocado relish (see recipe, page 104), a
mixed salad or cucumber and yogurt sauce
(see recipe, page 104).

chicken on a spit

This recipe is for those whose kitchen
equipment includes a rotisserie

1 medium-size chicken
3–4 teaspoons Dijon mustard
juice of 1–2 lemons
1–2 tablespoons olive oil
salt and pepper

Put the chicken on a plate and paint it all over
with the mustard. Squeeze the juice of
½ lemon over it. Sprinkle with salt and pepper,
and leave for 1 hour. Preheat the rotisserie.
Put the chicken on the spit and pour a little of
the olive oil over it. After a couple of minutes'
cooking, reduce the heat and then cook for a
good hour, basting with oil and lemon juice
frequently. Serve with rice and a lettuce
salad, with the pan juices in a sauce boat.

chaudfroid of chicken

one 3½ lb roasting chicken
1 onion
1 carrot
1 stalk celery
3 stalks parsley
½ bay leaf
5 tablespoons (⅝ stick) butter
4 tablespoons flour
2 envelopes (½ oz) powdered gelatine
1¼ cups heavy whipping cream
2–3 sprigs of fresh tarragon
1 small bunch chives
salt and 5 or 6 black peppercorns

SERVES 5–6

Bring 1 quart water with 1 teaspoon salt
to the boil. Poach the chicken with the onion,
carrot, and celery, cut in pieces and the
parsley, bay leaf and peppercorns, at a low
simmer, covered closely, for 1 hour. Lift out
the chicken and strain the stock, discarding
the vegetables. Cool the stock until the fat
has solidified on top. Remove every particle
of fat and boil up the stock until it is reduced
to 2½ cups. Melt the butter, stir in the flour
and cook for 2 minutes, stirring. Add 2 cups of
the stock gradually, stirring until smooth, and
simmer for 15 minutes, stirring occasionally.
Meanwhile dissolve the gelatine in the
remaining stock and add it to the sauce when
it has finished cooking. Stir until smooth,
then add the cream. When all is blended,
adjust the seasoning and pour into a bowl;
leave to cool until tepid and on the point of
setting. Carve the chicken into neat pieces,
removing all skin. Lay the pieces on a large
platter not touching each other. Spoon the
sauce over them allowing it to run smoothly of
its own accord, guiding with a spatula dipped
in hot water where necessary. Keep the bowl
of sauce warm over a pan of hot water, to
prevent it setting in the bowl, while the first
coating sets. Then make a second layer and
leave to set again. Decorate with the tarragon
leaves and the chives, cut in short lengths.
Chill in the refrigerator for a couple of hours.
Cut around each piece carefully and lift with a
spatula onto a flat platter.

marinated chicken

6 chicken breasts, with wings attached
1 tablespoon Dijon mustard
⅝ cup sunflower seed oil, or other light oil
⅝ cup yogurt
1 small piece (½ oz) fresh green ginger
½ teaspoon cumin seeds (whole or ground)
½ teaspoon coriander seeds (whole or ground)
½ teaspoon ground turmeric
juice of 1 lemon
1 green chili pepper

SERVES 6

Put the mustard in a bowl and add the oil,
drop by drop, whisking. When all is absorbed,
beat the yogurt until smooth, and stir in.
Chop the ginger and put in a mortar with the
coriander and cumin seeds and turmeric;
pound to a powder. Add the lemon juice and
stir to form a paste. Stir into the yogurt
mixture. Finely mince the chili pepper, and
add. Alternatively, this can be done very
quickly in a food processor. Make small cuts
all over the chicken pieces with the tip of a
sharp knife. Cover with the marinade
mixture. Leave for 6–24 hours in the
refrigerator. Preheat oven to 400°F. Lay the
chicken pieces in a shallow oiled baking pan
and bake for 35 minutes. Rearrange the
pieces from time to time so that they brown
evenly all over. This is good served with
boiled rice and cucumber and yogurt sauce
(see recipe, page 104).

chicken pâté

one 3½ lb chicken
¾ lb ground pork
¾ lb fresh pork fat, ground
½ lb fat bacon, blanched
1 medium-size onion
pinch of mace
4 tablespoons brandy
1 large egg
coarse salt and coarsely ground black pepper

SERVES 10–12

Make at least two days in advance of serving. Cut the uncooked chicken off the bones, discard the skin and chop the meat. Put in a large mixing bowl. (Reserve the bones to make stock.) Cut a few long thin strips of bacon fat and reserve; chop the rest in small dice and add. Chop the onion finely and add. Add the ground pork and pork fat, and mix all together, adding lots of salt and very coarsely ground black pepper, and a pinch of mace. Stir in the brandy. Fry a tiny ball of the mixture and taste to test for seasonings. Lightly beat the egg and stir in. Preheat oven to 325°F. Line an ovenproof dish or meat loaf pan with the strips of bacon fat, and fill with the mixture. Cover the pâté with foil and stand in a baking pan; pour in enough hot water to come halfway up the sides of the pâté pan. Bake for 2 hours and 10 minutes, or until the pâté has shrunk away from the sides of the pan. Cool for 1 hour, then put a 3lb weight on top and refrigerate. This pâté will keep for eight or nine days under refrigeration, or longer if additionally sealed with a layer of fat or clarified butter. This quantity can be made in two containers, in which case reduce baking time by about 25 minutes.

chicken mold

one 3½–4lb roasting chicken
1 onion
1 carrot
1 stalk celery
3 stalks parsley
½ bay leaf
5 or 6 black peppercorns
2 envelopes (½ oz) powdered gelatine
⅝ cup heavy whipping cream
3 sprigs fresh tarragon
small bunch of chives

SERVES 4–6

Start preparing 36 hours ahead. Bring 1 quart water with 1 teaspoon salt to the boil. Poach the chicken with the onion, carrot and celery, cut in pieces, and the parsley, bay leaf, salt and peppercorns, at a low simmer, covered closely for 1 hour. Cook 10 minutes longer for a 4lb chicken or one that is cold from the refrigerator. Lift out the chicken and strain the stock, discarding the vegetables. Cool the stock, then chill overnight in the refrigerator. The next day, remove every trace of fat and boil up the stock gently until it is reduced to 1¼ cups. Dissolve the gelatine in a little of the stock, then mix with the rest. Stir in the cream and add salt and pepper to taste. Pour into a bowl and leave to cool, stirring often to prevent a skin forming. Carve the chicken off the bone into neat slices, removing all skin. Lay the slices in a shallow dish which fits them nicely. When the stock-gelatine mixture is cool and about to set, pour it over the chicken. Refrigerate until set. Cut the chives into short lengths and decorate the dish with the cut-up chives and the tarragon sprigs.

Meat/lamb

braised lamb with vegetables

1 *shoulder of lamb*
1 *large onion*
¾ *lb carrots*
¾ *lb leeks*
6 *stalks celery*
2 *small turnips*
6 *tablespoons (¾ stick) butter*
1½ *tablespoons flour*
1 *egg yolk*
4 *tablespoons cream*
2 *tablespoons chopped parsley*
salt and pepper
SERVES 6

Have a casserole or heavy pot, with a lid, big enough to hold the shoulder. If necessary, ask the butcher to cut off the bone to make it less bulky. Chop the vegetables. Gently heat 4 tablespoons butter in the casserole and add the vegetables; cook for 5 minutes, stirring often. Take out the vegetables and put the lamb in; brown it on all sides. Put back the vegetables and pour in enough very hot water to come level with the surface of the lamb. Cover and simmer gently for 2 hours, either on top of the stove or in a low oven. When it is cooked, take out the meat and keep hot. Pour the vegetables and the liquid into a strainer over a bowl. Keep the vegetables hot but leave the stock to cool slightly while you carve the meat. Lay the slices on a large platter and surround with the vegetables. Cover with foil and keep warm. Skim off all the fat from the surface of the stock and measure 2½ cups. Melt the remaining butter in a small pan, stir in the flour, and then blend in the measured stock. Add salt and pepper to taste. Beat the egg yolk with the cream in a small bowl and stir in a little of the sauce. Return to the rest of the sauce in the pan and stir over very low heat until slightly thickened. Stir in the parsley. Serve the meat on a heated platter with a little of the sauce poured over it. Serve the rest of the sauce separately in a sauce boat.

navarin d'agneau

2½ *lb lean lamb, without bone*
2 *tablespoons beef drippings, bacon fat, or butter*
1¼ *cups chicken or beef stock*
1¼ *cups white wine*
1¼ *cups mixed vegetable juice*
½ *lb small new potatoes*
½ *lb very small onions*
½ *lb small carrots*
½ *lb turnips*
½ *lb zucchini squash*
½ *lb green beans*
¼ *lb shelled peas*
3 *tablespoons butter*
3 *tablespoons flour*
4 *tablespoons chopped parsley*
salt and pepper
SERVES 4–5

Cut the lamb in neat cubes. Melt the drippings, bacon fat or butter in a heavy casserole and brown the meat in it. Mix the stock, wine and vegetable juice and heat in a separate pan. Pour over the meat and stir until simmering. Cover the pan and cook gently for 1 hour. Peel the potatoes, onions, carrots and turnips, leaving them whole, and add. Bring back to simmering point, cover the pan and simmer for another 30 minutes. Add the zucchini cut in thick chunks with the skin on, and the green beans and the peas. After 30 minutes mix the flour and butter to a paste and drop into the pan in small bits, stirring until each one is amalgamated. Add salt and pepper to taste and sprinkle with the chopped parsley. Accompany with French bread.

barbecued skewers of lamb

½ leg of lamb, boned

SERVES 4–6

The day before, or at least six hours in advance, cut the lamb in neat evenly sized cubes, fairly small. Mix together a little oil, lemon juice, salt, pepper and a dash of Tabasco, and pour over the lamb in a bowl. Leave overnight, or for several hours, turning now and then. When the barbecue or broiler is hot, thread the lamb pieces onto skewers, being careful not to crowd them. Grill them slowly, basting with the remaining sauce until well browned outside but still pink inside.

carré d'agneau

1 rack of lamb (seven ribs)
1 glass dry red wine

SERVES 3–4

Preheat the oven to 375°F. Lay the lamb on a rack in a roasting pan, cover loosely with a piece of foil, and put in the oven. After half an hour, remove the pan from the oven, and lower the heat to about 340°F. Remove the foil, pour a glass of dry red wine over the meat, and replace in the oven, baste two or three times during the remainder of the cooking time, 1 hour in all. Leave in a warm place for 10 minutes before carving into chops. Scrape the juices together over a low flame and pour into a sauce boat.

Irish stew

2½ lb stewing lamb, cut in pieces
2 lb potatoes
1 lb mild onions, sliced
2 tablespoons parsley
salt and pepper

SERVES 4–5

Peel and slice the onions and potatoes, cutting about half the potatoes in thicker slices and the rest in fine slices. Put the potatoes, lamb and onions in layers in a heavy casserole, seasoning each layer with salt and pepper. Use the thicker potato slices in the upper layers. Add 2 cups of hot water, and bring to the boil. Lower the heat, cover and simmer for 2–2½ hours; or place, covered, in an oven preheated to 310°F, for the same length of time. When cooked, half the potatoes should have dissolved to thicken the sauce, while the thicker-cut ones should retain their shape.

lamb loaf with tomatoes

2 lb ground lamb
1 large onion
4 tablespoons finely chopped parsley
one 8oz can Italian tomatoes
pinch of sugar
salt and freshly ground black pepper

SERVES 5–6

Put the ground lamb in a large bowl and add plenty of salt and freshly ground black pepper. Finely chop the onion and the parsley, and add; mix very well. Spread the mixture in a shallow layer in a greased baking pan about 10 inches square. Preheat oven to 350°F. Pour the tomatoes into a bowl and chop them roughly with the blade of a spatula. Add the sugar and some salt and pepper. Pour the tomato mixture over the meat and bake for 1 hour. When ready, the meat will have shrunk away from the sides of the pan and there will be a lot of pan juices. Extract these with a baster, skim, and keep hot. To serve, cut the lamb loaf into fairly thick sections and serve with the hot pan juices poured generously over them.

yogurtliya

This Turkish dish, which I first ate in Istanbul, is quickly assembled and made, but should not be left long before being eaten. Like many Middle Eastern dishes, it is served warm rather than hot

½ *lb lean tender lamb*

1 *tablespoon sunflower seed oil, or other light oil*

3 *tablespoons butter*

2 *large pieces pita bread*

1 *lb tomatoes*

1¼ *cups yogurt, at room temperature*

1 *oz shelled pine nuts*

2 *tablespoons chopped parsley*

coarse salt and freshly ground black pepper

SERVES 4

Cut the meat in small neat cubes and sauté until cooked through in a mixture of the oil and 2 tablespoons of the butter. Keep hot. Split the pita and cut in triangles; toast lightly under the broiler until pale golden. Peel the tomatoes and chop coarsely. Sauté them very briefly in the remaining 1 tablespoon butter, stopping as soon as they are softened but before they have turned into a mush. Beat the yogurt well and season to taste with the sea salt and black pepper. Lay some of the bread pieces on a large platter and pour the tomatoes over them with their juices. Pour most of the yogurt over the tomatoes, reserving a little. Drain the meat of its cooking juices and lay over the top, surround with more triangles of bread and sprinkle with the pine nuts and chopped parsley. Serve with a crisp lettuce salad.

barbecued leg of lamb

1 *small leg of lamb, boned*

1 *teaspoon olive oil*

coarse salt and coarsely ground black pepper

SERVES 5–6

Ask the butcher to cut the lamb so as to give you a rectangular piece of meat of roughly even thickness. Sprinkle with freshly ground black pepper and lay, fat side down, facing the heat, on the grill. Barbecue for about 12 minutes, then brush some olive oil over the uncooked side, turn and grill for another 10–15 minutes. Do not let it become too black. To serve, lift it onto a board and cut in fairly thick slices. It should still be quite pink within. Serve with coarse salt.

spicy meat balls

1½ *lb ground lamb*

1 *medium-size onion*

1 *teaspoon ground coriander*

1 *teaspoon ground cumin*

½ *teaspoon chili powder*

4 *tablespoons very finely chopped parsley*

1 *tablespoon oil*

1 *tablespoon butter*

coarse salt and freshly ground black pepper

SERVES 4

Mince or finely chop the onion and mix it with the meat. Add a good quantity of coarse salt and freshly ground black pepper, and stir in the spices and the finely chopped parsley; mix, and form into very small balls. Lay the balls on a floured surface until ready to cook. Heat the oil and butter in a heavy pan and when very hot put in as many of the balls as you can cook at one time without crowding. Turn on all sides until evenly brown, then drain on paper towels and keep hot while you cook the rest. Serve with a mixed salad.

Meat/beef and pork

broiled sirloin with garnishes

This is a good dish for dieters

1 *sirloin steak about 1½ inches thick*
2 *oz tiny onions*
¼ *lb button mushrooms*
½ *bunch watercress*
4 *small tomatoes*
1½ *lemons*
SERVES 4

Broil the steak at high heat until well browned outside but still red within, about 4–5 minutes on each side. Cool. Peel and cook the onions in boiling water until tender; drain and cool. Clean and slice the mushrooms. Divide the watercress into tender sprigs and wash. Slice the tomatoes. Cut the cold beef in diagonal slices and divide among four plates, garnishing with the cooked onions, sliced mushrooms, watercress sprigs and sliced tomatoes. Squeeze the lemon juice over the vegetables. Serve with horseradish sauce (see recipe, page 107).

barbecued spareribs

This amount is enough for 4 people as part of a larger meal, but as a main course, you will need 1 lb per person. Racks of ribs can be cooked on a spit threaded concertina fashion, or spread out in baking pans and baked in a hot oven (450°F) for 1 hour

2 *lb spareribs*
barbecue sauce 2 (see recipe, page 108)
SERVES 4

Keep the spareribs whole, in racks; brush them with the sauce and leave them for 1 hour before cooking. Grill gently, basting often with the sauce as the spareribs cook, for about 15 minutes on each side; be careful not to let them burn. Cut them into ribs and serve with the sauce poured over.

skewered plums with bacon

6 *large or 12 small ripe plums*
6 *slices bacon*
SERVES 4

Remove the seeds from the plums, cutting them in half if they are large. Cut each slice of bacon in half and wrap around a plum, or half a plum, according to size. Thread three on each of four small skewers and broil slowly, turning often, until the bacon is crisp – about 10 minutes. These are delicious when served with broiled pork chops, broiled sausages, broiled chicken, roast turkey or goose, or roast game birds of any sort.

barbecued ham steaks

4 *ham steaks, ready-to-eat*
barbecue sauce 2 (see recipe, page 108)
SERVES 4

Coat the steaks on each side with the sauce, and leave to marinate for 1 or 2 hours before grilling. Grill for 4–5 minutes on each side, basting often with the marinade. Serve with the sauce poured over.

pork and spinach loaf

¾ *lb pure pork sausage meat*
1½ *lb spinach*
½ *lb pastry (see recipe, page 126)*
1 *egg yolk*
salt and pepper
SERVES 3–4

Cook the spinach briefly in ½–⅔ cup boiling water, drain well, squeeze out as much moisture as possible and chop. Make the pastry; enclose it in plastic wrap and refrigerate for 30 minutes. Roll it out on a floured surface to form a rectangle. Form the sausage meat into a fat roll a little shorter than the width of the pastry. Spoon the spinach onto the pastry in an even layer. Sprinkle with salt and pepper. Lay the sausage roll on the spinach and roll up the pastry and spinach around it. Seal the edges with a little water. Preheat the oven to 350°F. Beat the egg yolk and brush it onto the pastry. Use the pastry trimmings to decorate the loaf. Lift the pastry-encased loaf carefully onto a buttered baking tray and bake for 45 minutes, then reduce the oven heat to 325°F and bake a further 30 minutes. If it seems to be getting too brown, cover loosely with a piece of foil. This is at its best hot, with mustard sauce (see recipe, page 106), but it can also be eaten cold, at a picnic, for example.

broiled loin of pork with sesame seeds

| 1 3–3½ lb boneless loin of pork |
| 2 tablespoons soy sauce |
| 2 tablespoons sweet vermouth or sherry |
| 1 tablespoon finely chopped shallots |
| 2 teaspoons sesame seeds |
| coarsely ground black pepper |
| SERVES 4–6 |

Make a marinade by mixing the soy sauce with the vermouth or sherry, and stirring in the chopped shallots. Cut the loin in neat slices about ¼ inch thick. Brush the slices on both sides with the marinade and leave for 1 or 2 hours. Put the slices of pork under the broiler and scatter over them half the sesame seeds. Broil slowly until well browned, about 5 minutes. Turn, and scatter over them the remaining sesame seeds. Broil another 4–5 minutes. Serve with coarse salt, mustard and a green salad, and a dish of noodles or hot rice.

broiled pork with ginger

| 1½ lb boneless pork |
| 6 tablespoons pineapple juice |
| 3 tablespoons soy sauce |
| 2 tablespoons clear honey |
| 1 piece preserved ginger |
| SERVES 3–4 |

Mix the fruit juice with the soy sauce and the honey. Wash the ginger briefly to remove the syrup, then chop it finely and stir into the marinade. Cut the pork in thin slices, removing as much of the fat as possible, and lay the slices between two pieces of plastic wrap. Beat with a mallet until very thin. Lay in a shallow dish and pour the marinade over them. Leave for 1 hour, turning occasionally. When the broiler is hot, remove the pork from the marinade and lay it on a rack in a broiling pan. Remove the little pieces of ginger from the marinade with a teaspoon and reserve them. Broil the pork, brushing with extra marinade once or twice, for about 4 minutes on each side. Be careful that it does not burn. Serve with the ginger scattered over the meat. Accompany with boiled rice and a green salad.

barbecued pork chops

| 4 large pork chops |
| barbecue sauce 2 (see recipe, page 108) |
| SERVES 4 |

Coat the chops on both sides with the sauce. Leave them to marinate for at least an hour before cooking. Baste with more of the sauce while grilling, being careful not to let them become too blackened; they should be cooked slowly and thoroughly. Serve with coarse salt and mustard.

mushroom koulibiac

In England, frozen puff pastry is available and I find it satisfactory. In the United States it is hard to find, but uncooked puff pastry can be purchased from some bakeries. Otherwise make your own using your favorite recipe

4 *tablespoons rice*
4 *eggs* + 1 *yolk*
¾ *lb mushrooms*
⅝ *cup (1¼ stick) butter*
juice of ½ lemon
1 *lb puff pastry*
salt and pepper
SERVES 6

Cook the rice in plenty of boiling salted water (about 3 cups) until tender. Hard boil the eggs, shell and chop them. Wipe the mushrooms and slice them thickly. Heat 4 tablespoons butter in a frying pan and sauté the mushrooms for about 2 minutes. Add the lemon juice, cover the pan and cook gently another 10 minutes. Slowly heat the remaining butter in a clean pan. Roll out the pastry in two rectangles or squares on a floured surface. Add the remaining melted butter to the rice with salt and pepper. Preheat oven to 400°F. Put a layer of the rice mixture on one pastry rectangle. Sprinkle half the chopped hard-boiled eggs onto the mixture, then add the mushrooms, drained of their juice. Add a layer of the remaining eggs, then the rest of the rice. Cover with the second piece of pastry and seal the edges firmly. Beat the egg yolk and brush the pastry with it. Bake for 25 minutes, until brown. Serve with herb sauce (see recipe, page 105).

mushrooms in sour cream

1 *lb flat mushrooms*
4 *tablespoons (½ stick) butter*
1¼ *cups sour cream*
juice of ½ lemon
2 *tablespoons chopped chervil or dill (optional)*
salt and pepper

Wipe the mushrooms and cut off the stalks. Slice the caps and sauté them gently in the butter. When they have softened, after about 8 minutes, stir in the sour cream and mix well, adding salt, pepper and a little lemon juice to taste. Stir until reheated and serve with noodles or boiled rice. If you wish, chopped fresh chervil or dill can be added at the last moment to give extra flavor.

mushrooms in pastry cases

1 *lb short pastry (see recipe, page 126)*
1½ *lb flat mushrooms*
6 *tablespoons (¾ stick) butter*
1 *tablespoon flour*
1¼ *cups chicken stock*
⅝ *cup sour cream*
juice of ½ lemon
1 *tablespoon chopped parsley*
1 *egg yolk*
salt and pepper
SERVES 6–8

Make the pastry, then chill for 30 minutes. Roll out thinly on a floured surface and divide to line 6–8 small round tart pans. Preheat the oven to 375°F. Put a tiny piece of greased foil in each one of the pans and lay a few pastry trimmings on top. Bake for 10 minutes. Take out the foil and scraps and return to the oven for another 5 minutes. Cool. Use only the caps of the mushrooms; slice them and sauté gently in 4 tablespoons of the butter in a frying pan, stirring. Drain off the juice.

Reserve the mushrooms. Melt the remaining 2 tablespoons butter and add the flour. Cook for 1 minute, stirring, then add the heated stock and the sour cream. Simmer for 3 minutes, stirring. Add salt and pepper to taste and lemon juice. Stir in the cooked mushrooms and the chopped parsley. Brush the pastry cases all over with beaten egg yolk and put back in the oven for 5 minutes to glaze. Take them out and fill with the mushroom mixture. Serve immediately.

mushroom pudding

This unusual suet pudding is delicious served with stewed beef, carrots and onions

2 *cups self-rising flour*
4 *oz ground suet*
¾ *lb small button mushrooms*
2 *tablespoons butter*
juice of ½ *lemon*
⅝ *cup chicken stock*
salt and pepper
SERVES 4

To make pastry: sift the flour, add a pinch of salt and mix in the ground suet. Add enough ice water to make a thick paste. Cut in two uneven pieces and roll out the larger one thinly to line a 3¾-cup capacity heatproof bowl. Wipe and trim the mushroom caps and put them in the bowl with the butter cut in small pieces. Add salt and pepper, then add the lemon juice and the stock. Roll out the remaining pastry to form a lid, lay over the top and trim and seal the edges. Cover with a greased piece of aluminum foil and tie with string. Place in a large pan half-full of boiling water, cover the pan and steam the pudding for at least 2½ hours.

stuffed Chinese cabbage

1 *head Chinese cabbage*
⅔ *cup rice*
1 *bunch scallions*
4 *tablespoons chopped herbs: chervil, parsley, tarragon, dill*
6 *hard-boiled eggs*
2½ *cups chicken stock*
salt and pepper
SERVES 6

Separate the leaves of the cabbage and choose the six best ones. Make sure that they are large but tender. Cut the rest in strips. Put the whole leaves into a large pan with 2 quarts of boiling water and boil for 1 minute; remove leaves carefully and drain. Put the rice into the same boiling water and cook for 5 minutes; drain. Slice the scallions, chop the herbs and mix with the rice, adding salt and pepper to taste. Spread out each leaf carefully and put a mound of rice on each one. Lay a whole hard-boiled egg in the center and wrap the leaves up carefully. Place a layer of shredded cabbage in a broad, shallow oiled pan and lay the stuffed leaves among them. Heat the stock and pour over the cabbage rolls. Bring to boiling point, reduce heat, cover the pan and simmer for 30 minutes. They can be served hot: with the extra leaves and moistened with their juice, or cold: lifted out of the pan and laid on a flat platter to cool. Moisten with some of the juice after cooling and use the rest of the cabbage and juice to make a delicious soup. In either case, serve with lemon wedges.

cabbage timbale

1 *small green cabbage*
1 *lb potatoes*
4 *tablespoons (½ stick) butter*
4 *eggs*
salt and pepper
SERVES 4–5

Cut the cabbage into pieces, wash well and drop into boiling salted water. Cook for 8 minutes or until tender, drain well and chop finely. Boil the potatoes, then press them through a coarse-mesh sieve or use a food processor to make a puree. Put this puree in a heavy pan and stir over a low heat to dry it. Beat in the butter in small pieces, while the potato is still hot, and add salt and pepper to taste. Stir in the chopped cabbage and taste again for seasoning. Preheat the oven to 325°F. Separate the eggs, beat the yolks until stiff and fold in. Spoon the mixture into a buttered soufflé dish and place in a baking pan half-full of hot water. Bake for 40 minutes until lightly colored and firm. Serve with hot tomato sauce 1 (see recipe, page 103).

lettuce puree

This delicious puree can be served with roast chicken, poached or grilled fish

2 *large heads lettuce*
1 *small bunch scallions, or ½ medium-size onion*
6 *tablespoons (¾ stick) butter*
2 *tablespoons flour*
1¼ *cups cream*
pinch of mace or nutmeg
salt and pepper
SERVES 3–4

Cut the lettuces in quarters, wash well and put into boiling water; cook for 5 minutes. Drain well and chop finely. Dry out by stirring over gentle heat for a few moments in a heavy pan. Slice the scallions (or chop the half onion) and sauté gently in 2 tablespoons butter in a small covered pan for 5 minutes, stirring occasionally. Melt the remaining 4 tablespoons butter in a saucepan, stir in the flour, blend, then add the heated cream. Stir until blended, adding salt and pepper to taste, and a pinch of mace or nutmeg. Stir in the scallions and the chopped lettuce, and adjust the seasoning to taste.

vegetable fritters

1 *small eggplant*
2 *medium-size zucchini squash*
2 *tomatoes*
1 *cup flour*
2 *tablespoons sunflower seed oil, or other light oil*
⅝ *cup soda water*
1 *egg white*
salt
SERVES 4

Cut the unpeeled eggplant and zucchini in thin diagonal slices. Cut the tomatoes vertically also in thin slices. (The tomatoes should be firm, not too juicy.) Make the batter. Sift the flour with a pinch of salt into a mixing bowl. Stir in the oil and the soda water (if necessary, ordinary water may be used). You should have a batter the consistency of fairly thick cream. Heat a pan of deep oil to 360°F. Fold the stiffly beaten egg white into the batter and use immediately: dip the vegetable slices into the batter and shake off any excess. Drop them into the oil, and turn them over as soon as they are golden brown on one side. They should be done in small batches – on no account crowd them in the pan. As soon as they are brown on both sides, drain them on paper towels. Serve hot, with skordalia (see recipe, page 104).

spiced zucchini

This is good with lamb and pork dishes

¾ lb zucchini squash

2 tablespoons butter

1 tablespoon sunflower seed oil

½ lb tomatoes

½ teaspoon ground cumin

½ teaspoon ground coriander

salt and pepper

SERVES 4

Cut the unpeeled zucchini in ½-inch slices. Heat the butter and oil in a frying pan. Put in the zucchini and sauté gently with the lid on for 8 minutes, stirring now and then. Peel and roughly chop the tomatoes, and add with salt and pepper and the spices. Cover again and cook for another 8 minutes. Leave for 5 minutes in a warm place before serving.

cucumbers stuffed with green rice

Green rice also makes an excellent stuffing for cold tomatoes

2 cucumbers

⅔ cup long-grain rice

2 tablespoons olive oil

1 tablespoon white wine vinegar

6 tablespoons chopped herbs: parsley, chives, tarragon, chervil, dill

salt and pepper

SERVES 4

Cook the rice in plenty of boiling salted water (about 2 cups) until tender and drain immediately. Add salt and pepper to taste, then stir in the oil and vinegar. Leave to cool, then stir in the chopped herbs. Peel the cucumbers and cut in half lengthwise. Cut across in 2-inch pieces, then shape each one roughly to form a sort of boat, hollowing out the interior and rounding the ends. Sprinkle the interiors with salt and stand upside down to drain for 30 minutes. Pat dry with paper towels and fill each one with the green rice.

stuffed eggplants

4 medium-size eggplants

4 tablespoons (½ stick) butter

1 medium-size onion

1 clove garlic, finely minced

1½ lb ground lamb

3 tomatoes

1½ tablespoons flour

1¼ cups milk

4 tablespoons grated cheese

salt and pepper

SERVES 4

Bake the eggplants for 30 minutes in the oven preheated to 350°F. Cool slightly, then cut a thin sliver off the top surface. Scoop out the pulp with a small spoon, trying not to break through the skin. Set aside the pulp for another dish. Chop the onion and cook gently in 2 tablespoons of the butter until pale golden. Add the minced garlic and the meat and stir around until nicely browned on all sides. Season well with salt and pepper. Leave to cool slightly, then spoon the mixture into the eggplant shells. Peel the tomatoes, slice them thinly and lay over the meat. Preheat the oven to 375°F. Make a cheese sauce: melt 2 tablespoons butter, add the flour and cook, stirring, for 1 minute. Add the milk, stirring as the sauce thickens. Add the cheese and stir in. Season to taste. The sauce should be very thick. Spoon over the stuffed eggplants in their baking dish. Bake for 10–15 minutes until well browned. These are very filling and extremely rich and only need a crisp green salad as accompaniment.

eggplant spread

Serve on small squares of rye bread or pumpernickel, or with crackers as a snack with drinks

1½ lb small eggplants
1 small onion
4 tablespoons olive oil
1 clove garlic, finely chopped
½ lb tomatoes
pinch of sugar
1–2 tablespoons lemon juice
salt and pepper
SERVES 6–8

Preheat oven to 400°F. Bake the eggplants whole until soft, 45–60 minutes. Test by piercing with a cooking fork. When soft, take them out and leave to cool. Chop the onion and put it in a frying pan with half the oil. Sauté until lightly colored, adding the garlic halfway through. Put to one side. Peel and finely chop the tomatoes. Cut the eggplants in half and scrape out the inner pulp; put the pulp in a bowl and mix with the tomatoes, and the fried onion. Add salt and black pepper to taste, and the pinch of sugar. Heat the remaining 2 tablespoons oil in the frying pan and sauté the eggplant mixture gently for about 30 minutes, stirring now and then. By the end of the cooking time it should be quite thick. Remove from the heat and stir in lemon juice to taste. Cool and chill in the refrigerator for several hours before serving.

celery hearts mornay

1 large can celery hearts
8 slices ham
3 tablespoons butter
2½ tablespoons flour
2 cups chicken or vegetable stock
⅝ cup cream
1¼ cups grated Gruyère cheese
salt and pepper
SERVES 4

Divide the celery hearts into 8 pieces and roll each one in a slice of ham. Lay the rolls in a buttered ovenproof dish. Preheat the oven to 350°F. Melt the butter, stir in the flour and blend with 2 cups chicken or vegetable stock. When blended, add the cream and season with salt and pepper. Shake in the cheese, reserving a little for the top, and stir. When smooth and blended, pour the sauce over the rolls. Scatter the remaining cheese over the top and bake in the oven for 30 minutes. Serve with a crisp green salad.

potato cake with onions

1½ lb potatoes, freshly cooked and mashed
2 large onions
4 tablespoons (½ stick) butter
salt and pepper
SERVES 4

Slice the onions thinly. Melt 3 tablespoons of the butter in a frying pan and fry the onions briskly until well browned, even slightly burned in places. Stir the onion into the hot mashed potato, scraping up all the brown bits, and season with plenty of salt and pepper. Melt the remaining butter in the frying pan, and spread the potato and onion mixture evenly over the whole surface of the pan. Cook gently for about 25 minutes, then turn onto a platter; it should have a nicely browned crust. Cut in wedges like a cake, and serve with bacon and eggs or cold meat and salad.

potato puree with chervil

This is good with roast or broiled chicken, escalopes of veal, trout or poached eggs

1½ lb potatoes
⅝ cup milk
4 tablespoons (½ stick) butter
2 tablespoons cream
4 tablespoons chopped chervil
salt and pepper
SERVES 4

Peel the potatoes, cut in pieces and boil them briefly, until tender. Drain and dry out slightly over a low heat. Press through a medium-mesh sieve into a heavy pan or put in a food processor to make a dry puree. Put the milk in a small pan with the butter and cream, and plenty of salt and pepper. Heat until the butter has melted. Add the chervil and mix. Put the potato pan over gentle heat and add the liquid mixture gradually, beating it in. When all the liquid is absorbed you should have a smooth creamy puree flecked with green. Pour into a heated serving dish.

potato pancakes

These are best served with cold meat, bacon and eggs, or ham. Do not prepare them in advance; the mixture will discolor if kept waiting, and it is best to serve them immediately after they have been cooked

1 lb potatoes
1 onion
2 eggs
2 tablespoons flour
1 tablespoon sunflower seed oil, or other light oil
salt and pepper
SERVES 4–6

Grate the raw potatoes quite finely, so that they form thin strips. Grate the onion. Beat the eggs and mix with the potato and onion in a large bowl. Sift the flour and add, with salt and pepper. Heat a thin layer of oil in a large frying pan or griddle. When it is very hot, put in three large spoonfuls of the mixture and flatten them with a spatula to form roughly round shapes. They need about 5 minutes cooking on each side; do not let them brown too quickly, as the raw potato strips must have time to cook properly.

chasse

This is an old-fashioned English breakfast dish, but also makes a good high tea or light supper dish. It is delicious served with poached eggs on top

1 large onion
3 tablespoons butter
¾ lb tomatoes
1 thick slice ham, 5–6 oz
½ lb potatoes
2 tablespoons chopped parsley
salt and pepper
SERVES 3–4

Chop the onion. Melt the butter in a frying pan and sauté the onion until it starts to color. Peel and chop the tomatoes and dice the ham; add both to the pan. In the meantime, cook the potatoes in boiling salted water until just tender, then drain and chop. After the mixture in the frying pan has cooked for a few moments, add the chopped potatoes and about 4 tablespoons boiling water. (If the tomatoes are very juicy, the water may not be needed.) Cook for about ten minutes more, until the potatoes are completely soft and the liquid absorbed. Sprinkle with the chopped parsley and serve with or without poached eggs on top.

Vegetables/peas and beans

fresh pease pudding

Serve with hot or cold ham, roast pork, or sausages of any kind

2½ lb old peas, weighed in the pod

pinch of sugar

2 tablespoons chopped fresh mint

3 tablespoons butter

salt and pepper

SERVES 3–4

Shell the peas and put them in a bowl lined with cheesecloth. Add salt and pepper and a pinch of sugar. Stir in the chopped mint and tie up the cheesecloth with a piece of string. Bring a large pan of stock or water to the boil and lower the bundle of peas into the boiling liquid. Bring back to the boil, reduce heat, cover and simmer for 1 hour. Lift out the pudding bundle and stand in a colander. Cool for a few minutes, then untie the cloth. Puree the contents in a food processor, or press through a coarse sieve. Put back into the cloth and re-form into a round ball. Turn out on a shallow platter. Heat the butter until melted and pour it over the pudding. This is also good served cold. In this case, cut in slices and serve with melted butter.

lentils and buttermilk

½ lb lentils

3¾ cups chicken stock

2½ cups buttermilk

juice of ½ lemon

salt and pepper

SERVES 4–5

Put the lentils in the cold stock, bring to the boil, and simmer for about 45 minutes or until tender, adding salt and pepper to taste toward the end of the cooking time. Pour the cold buttermilk into a bowl and stir in the whole lentils with their liquid. Add lemon juice to taste. I like to eat this immediately, with the contrast of the hot lentils and the cold buttermilk, but it is also good after cooling. To make an unusual cold soup, puree in the blender and thin with stock, as required.

barbecued corn on the cob

Method 1: fold back the outer leaves (husks) from the ear of corn and remove, with the silky inner covering. Cut away all the cornsilk from the green-leaf husks. Spread butter on each ear and replace inside the husk; enclose the ear with the leaves and lay on the grill. Barbecue for 15–20 minutes, turning frequently. Serve with extra butter.

Method 2: remove husk and silk completely and discard. Wash the ear of corn and dry in a cloth. Spread butter on the ear and wrap tightly in a double thickness of foil. Lay directly on the coals and cook for 15–20 minutes, turning several times. Serve with extra slightly melted butter.

a vegetable hors d'oeuvre

½ lb green beans

¾ lb tomatoes

½ lb mushrooms

2 tablespoons olive oil

2 teaspoons white wine vinegar

salt and pepper

SERVES 4

Peel and slice the tomatoes. Wipe and slice the mushrooms. Cut the ends from the beans and put them in boiling salted water. Cook briefly and drain. While the beans are still warm, arrange them with the tomatoes and mushrooms on a large platter or on three separate dishes. Mix the oil and vinegar with salt and pepper and pour over all.

tomato sauce 1

one 16 oz can peeled tomatoes
1 tablespoon butter
pinch of sugar
dash of Tabasco
salt and pepper

Put the tomatoes with their juice in the blender, then pour the puree into a pan and heat. Add a little salt and pepper, a pinch of sugar and a dash of Tabasco. When boiling point is reached, add the butter and remove the sauce from the heat.

tomato sauce 2

This is good served with goujons of sole and other fish dishes

½ lb tomatoes
2 tablespoons sour cream
juice of ½ lemon
dash of Tabasco

Peel the tomatoes, cut in pieces and discard the seeds; put in the blender. Blend briefly, then add the sour cream and blend again. Add lemon juice to taste, and a dash of Tabasco. Pour into a shallow dish and freeze for 1½ hours, stirring once or twice. It should be served slightly thickened and very cold without being frozen solid.

tomato sauce 3

Serve with crudités such as cucumber, fennel, celery and scallions

⅝ cup mayonnaise
⅝ cup sour cream
2 tablespoons tomato paste
2 tablespoons lemon juice

Mix the mayonnaise and sour cream together, then beat in the tomato paste, and stir in the lemon juice a little at a time.

tomato and pepper sauce

Serve hot with noodles

3 tablespoons butter
1 small onion
1 teaspoon flour
one 8 oz can Italian plum tomatoes
two 4 oz jars or cans pimentos or sweet red peppers
pinch of sugar
1 tablespoon chopped basil or marjoram, or a handful of chopped chives
salt and pepper

Chop the onion finely. Melt the butter and sauté the onion until golden. Add the flour and stir; add the tomatoes with their juice and chop them up very roughly with a spatula. Cook for 3–4 minutes, stirring occasionally. Meanwhile drain and chop the peppers and add them to the mixture. Simmer for about 8 minutes, adding salt and pepper to taste, a pinch of sugar and the chopped fresh herbs and stir all together briefly.

tomato chili sauce

one 3 oz packet cream cheese
⅝ cup buttermilk
½ tablespoon lemon juice
generous ¼ cup tomato paste
¼ teaspoon Tabasco
salt and pepper

Put the cheese in a blender with the buttermilk. Blend until smooth, then add the lemon juice and salt and pepper to taste. Add the tomato paste and blend again. Then add the Tabasco, a drop at a time, until the required degree of hotness is reached.

mayonnaise

2 egg yolks, at room temperature
pinch of salt
pinch of mustard powder
1¼ cups olive oil
1½ tablespoons white wine vinegar
½ tablespoon lemon juice

MAKES ABOUT 1½ CUPS

Place the egg yolks in a large bowl, firmly anchored on a damp cloth so that it will not slide around. Add the salt and mustard powder. Break and stir the yolks with a wire whisk, then start adding the oil, drop by drop, beating all the time. After a moment or two the mixture will start to take on an emulsified appearance, like a thick ointment; now you can start to add the oil a little more quickly, in a very thin stream, beating constantly with the other hand. After half the oil is absorbed, the remainder can be added in a thin steady stream. Add a little of the vinegar from time to time. When all the oil is used up, add what is left of the vinegar, and the lemon juice. Keep in a cool place until needed, covered tightly with plastic wrap. The quantities can easily be doubled, but do not try to make half this amount, as it is likely to separate. If the sauce does separate, start again in a clean bowl, either by breaking in a fresh egg yolk, or a teaspoonful of Dijon mustard. Then add the separated sauce, drop by drop, then the remaining ingredients. Additions of chopped herbs or other ingredients should be stirred in at the very last; the sauce can be lightened by folding in a spoonful of whipped cream at the end. For tomato mayonnaise, peel, seed and puree ½ lb fresh tomatoes and stir them in at the end. For garlic mayonnaise, peel 2 cloves of garlic; pound to paste and add to the bowl at the start.

cucumber and yogurt sauce

Serve with broiled, barbecued or tandoori chicken

⅝ cup yogurt
1 large cucumber
dash of Tabasco
salt and pepper

Beat the yogurt until smooth. Peel the cucumber and cut it into small cubes. Stir into the yogurt, adding salt, pepper and Tabasco.

avocado relish

This makes a good accompaniment to chicken or any plain fish dish

2 avocados
juice of ½ lemon
½ lb tomatoes
1 bunch scallions
2 tablespoons sunflower seed oil, or other light oil
juice of 1 lime
pepper

Skin the avocados and cut in dice. Sprinkle them with lemon juice. Peel and chop the tomatoes, discarding seeds and juice. Mix with the avocado. Slice the scallions and mix in. Add pepper to taste. Dress with the oil, and 1 tablespoon of lime and lemon juice, mixed together.

skordalia

Serve with vegetable fritters

4 large cloves garlic
1 large potato
2 slices slightly stale bread
⅝ cup olive oil
juice of ½ lemon

SERVES 4–5

Crush the garlic and pound in a mortar. Boil and mash the potato, add it to the garlic and pound again. Cut the crusts off the bread and soak for 10 minutes in water. Squeeze it between your hands and add to the potato. Pound again until reduced to a smooth pulp. Add the oil drop by drop, beating it in with a wooden spoon. Be careful not to let it separate. When all is absorbed, add lemon juice to taste. Alternatively this can all be quickly done in a food processor.

herb sauce

This is good with crudités, new potatoes, baked potatoes or eggs

one 3 oz package cream cheese
⅝ cup buttermilk
juice of ½ lemon
4 tablespoons chopped herbs: chervil, tarragon, dill, chives
salt and pepper

Put the cheese in the blender with the buttermilk and blend until smooth. Add the lemon juice, and salt and pepper to taste. Stir in the herbs and serve cold.

shallot sauce

Serve with poached freshwater fish, such as trout, pike, or grayling

2 tablespoons chopped shallots
3 tablespoons chopped parsley
⅝ cup white wine
2 tablespoons butter
1 tablespoon flour
1¼ cups fish stock
2 tablespoons cream
salt and pepper

Put the chopped shallots and 2 tablespoons of the chopped parsley in a small pan with the wine. Bring to the boil, reduce heat and simmer, covered, for 3 minutes. Meanwhile

heat the fish stock, melt the butter in a saucepan, stir in the flour and cook for 1 minute, stirring. Gradually add the heated fish stock and cook for 3 minutes, stirring as it thickens. When smooth and blended, stir in the shallot mixture, then the cream. Add salt and pepper to taste, and the remaining tablespoon of chopped parsley.

ricotta sauce

Serve this delicious thick sauce with crudités such as tomatoes, celery or cauliflower

¼ lb ricotta cheese
⅝ cup yogurt
juice of ½ large lemon
2 tablespoons grated Parmesan cheese
2 tablespoons chopped parsley
pepper

Mix the ricotta with the yogurt until smooth. Add about 1½ tablespoons of lemon juice to taste, then stir in the grated Parmesan and chopped parsley. Add pepper to taste.

lemon butter

Use to baste all sorts of shellfish and other fish while grilling

½ cup (1 stick) sweet butter
2 tablespoons lemon juice
coarsely ground black pepper

Melt the butter, add the lemon juice and season with freshly ground coarse black pepper to taste.

tahini parsley sauce

Serve with cooked vegetables, crudités, chicken or white fish

⅝ cup tahini (sesame seed paste)

⅝ cup lemon juice

⅝ cup yogurt

4 tablespoons chopped parsley

1 teaspoon Dijon mustard (optional)

Put the tahini in a bowl and beat until smooth with a wooden spoon. Add the lemon juice gradually, beating all the time, then beat in the yogurt. Thin the mixture with a tablespoon of cold water if necessary. Add the mustard, if used, and stir in the chopped parsley and mix well.

pistou

This Mediterranean sauce is delicious served with young vegetables such as zucchini, small onions, new potatoes, broad beans, carrots, artichoke hearts. They should be freshly cooked and still warm

1¼ cups fresh basil leaves

2 cloves garlic

½ cup grated Parmesan cheese

1 large tomato

¾ cup olive oil

Chop the basil finely and pound in a mortar. Crush the garlic cloves and add to the mortar; pound again. Then add the grated cheese and continue to pound until a smooth paste. Turn on the broiler to high. Cut the tomato in half and broil the halves, flat surfaces up, close to the heat until they are almost blackened. Cool, remove the skin and chop. Add to the pistou and beat in. When smooth, add the oil, drop by drop, beating constantly, until all is well mixed together.

salsa verde

Serve with hot or cold boiled beef or bollito misto

1 egg yolk

1 tablespoon Dijon mustard

1 teaspoon sugar

2 cloves garlic, crushed

½ Spanish onion, finely chopped

1¼ cup chopped fresh herbs: parsley, chives, chervil, tarragon, dill

3 tablespoons white wine vinegar, or lemon juice

⅝ cup olive oil

2 hard-boiled eggs

salt and pepper

Beat the egg yolk in a large bowl with a whisk until smooth, adding the mustard, sugar, salt and pepper. Then add the crushed garlic, the finely chopped onion and the chopped herbs. Stir in the vinegar, or use lemon juice if you prefer, then oil. Lastly stir in the chopped hard-boiled eggs. Alternatively the whole sauce can be made in a food processor, which gives a smoother texture.

mustard sauce

Serve with cooked or raw vegetables, hard-boiled eggs, beef, chicken or fish salads

1 teaspoon Dijon mustard

1 tablespoon sour cream

⅝ cup yogurt

1–2 tablespoons lemon juice

pepper

Put the mustard in a bowl and beat in the sour cream. Add the yogurt, beat until blended and add lemon juice to taste and a little black pepper for extra flavor.

horseradish sauce

This is good served with hot or cold beef or with smoked fish

4 *tablespoons yogurt*

2 *tablespoons sour cream*

1 *tablespoon grated horseradish*

2 *teaspoons white wine vinegar*

pepper

Mix the yogurt with the sour cream, stir in the grated horseradish and vinegar and a little pepper according to taste.

green sauce

Serve with raw or cooked vegetables, especially cauliflower, green beans, tomatoes, new potatoes, cucumber or celery

1 *medium-size onion*

1 *tablespoon chopped parsley*

1 *teaspoon Dijon mustard*

1 *teaspoon sugar*

1 *large egg, at room temperature*

6 *tablespoons olive oil*

1 *tablespoon white wine vinegar*

1 *tablespoon lemon juice*

salt and pepper

Chop the onion and parsley very finely, stirring in the salt and pepper, mustard and sugar. Cook the egg at a bubbly simmer for exactly 5 minutes; shell. Cut it in half and stir the runny yolk into the sauce. Chop the white and add it also. Stir in the oil, vinegar and lemon juice, adding more vinegar if needed. Alternatively, the sauce can be made very quickly in a food processor: simply process the solid ingredients first, then add the oil, vinegar and lemon juice slowly through the hole in the lid.

shrimp sauce

Serve with any poached white fish, fish balls, or hard-boiled eggs

2½ *cups fresh shrimp, cooked*

1½ *tablespoons butter*

2 *teaspoons flour*

⅝ *cup cream*

1 *tablespoon finely chopped parsley*

pepper

Shell the shrimps and put the shells in a pan with cold water or fish stock to cover. Bring to the boil, reduce heat and simmer for at least 15 minutes, partially covered; strain and measure 1¼ cups of the liquid. Melt the butter, blend with the flour and cook, stirring, a minute or two; add the strained stock. Simmer until smooth and blended, stirring often, then add the cream. Blend again, and add the shrimps and pepper to taste. Keep just below simmering point for 3–4 minutes, until the shrimps are well heated, then sprinkle in the chopped parsley and serve.

curry sauce

Serve with freshwater fish such as cold poached trout or pike, or trout en gelée

¼ *teaspoon curry powder*

1 *egg yolk*

⅝ *cup olive oil*

2 *teaspoons white wine vinegar*

4 *tablespoons heavy whipping cream*

salt

Add the curry powder and a pinch of salt to the egg yolk in a mixing bowl and beat well. Add the oil drop by drop until starting to amalgamate, then in a very thin stream, stirring constantly. Thin the mayonnaise with the vinegar, as needed. Whip the cream and fold it in to make a light foamy sauce.

easy hollandaise sauce

This delicious sauce is time-consuming and tricky to make by traditional methods but can be made quickly and simply with a food processor. It can be made into sauce mousseline by adding 4 tablespoons of whipped cream at the last moment

3 *egg yolks*
½ *cup (1 stick) butter*
1 *tablespoon lemon juice*
pinch of salt

Warm the container of the food processor by filling it with very hot water and leaving it to stand for 2–3 minutes, then drain and dry it. Break in the egg yolks and add the salt. Turn on the processor, heat the butter in a small pan until bubbling, add the lemon juice and pour the mixture slowly through the hole in the lid of the processor. As soon as all the butter is amalgamated, switch off. Spoon into a warm sauce boat and serve immediately, or if it must be kept for a few minutes, stand it over a pan of very hot water. Do not on any account attempt to reheat the sauce.

egg sauce

This sauce can be enriched with cream and is delicious when served with any poached white fish, hot boiled ham, cauliflower or broccoli

2 *eggs*
1¼ *cups milk*
½ *bay leaf*
1 *slice onion*
1 *clove*
4 *tablespoons (½ stick) butter*
1½ *tablespoons flour*
pinch of mace or nutmeg
2 *tablespoons chopped parsley*
salt and pepper

Hard boil the eggs, and shell. Heat the milk in a small pan with the bay leaf, onion and clove. When simmering point is reached, remove from heat, cover the pan and leave for 20 minutes to flavor the milk. Melt the butter in a saucepan, add the flour and cook for 1 minute, stirring. Discard the bay leaf, onion and clove from the heated milk and add the milk to the saucepan. Stir until blended, add a pinch of mace or nutmeg, some salt and pepper and simmer for about 4 minutes. Chop the eggs and parsley and stir them in.

barbecue sauce 1

Use as a marinade and basting sauce for chicken

4 *tablespoons arachide oil, or peanut oil*
4 *tablespoons soy sauce*
4 *tablespoons vermouth*
1 *tablespoon finely chopped fresh ginger, or 1 piece washed and finely chopped preserved ginger*
2 *teaspoons finely chopped orange peel*
dash of Tabasco

Mix the oil with the soy sauce and the vermouth. Add the ginger, the orange peel and the Tabasco and mix well.

barbecue sauce 2

Use for marinating and basting pork

4 *tablespoons soy sauce*
2 *tablespoons brown sugar*
1 *tablespoon olive oil*
1 *large clove garlic*
1 *teaspoon fresh ginger, grated or chopped*
coarsely ground black pepper

Mix the soy sauce with the sugar, then stir in the oil. Crush or mince the garlic and add with the chopped or grated ginger. Add some coarsely ground black pepper and mix well.

Jams, relishes and pickles

plum jam

4 lb plums

8 cups (4 lb) sugar

Preheat oven to low, 275°F. Put the whole plums, stalks and seeds removed, in a large pot with 2½ cups water. Cover the pot and put in the oven for 2 hours. Put the sugar in a heavy pan. Add the cooked plums and their juice and stir; bring slowly to the boil. Boil fast for about 7–8 minutes, until setting point is reached. Skim, pour into hot sterilized jars and leave to cool before covering.

rhubarb and ginger jam

This jam is especially good with homemade white bread and butter. A cheaper version of ginger can be made by substituting 2 oz fresh root ginger, crushed and bruised and tied in a muslin bag, for the preserved ginger. This should be removed before bottling

4 lb rhubarb

6 cups (3 lb) sugar

3–4 lemons

3 tablespoons syrup from preserved ginger

2 oz (about 4 pieces) preserved ginger, finely sliced

Cut the rhubarb in small pieces and put in layers in a large dish, alternating with layers of sugar. Leave until the next day. Put in a heavy pan with all the juice. Peel off the zest of the lemons with a vegetable peeler and cut in thin strips. Add it to the rhubarb with the juice. Add the ginger syrup (or the root ginger) and bring slowly to the boil. Stir frequently until the sugar has dissolved, then boil rapidly for 15–20 minutes, until it sets. Skim, stir in the finely sliced preserved ginger (if using), and spoon into warm jars. Leave to cool, cover with greaseproof paper and screw-on lids.

apple and quince jelly

This makes a good alternative to red currant jelly for serving with lamb

6 lb apples

2 lb quinces

about 10 cups (5 lb) sugar

3 lemons

Wash the apples and quinces and cut them in quarters. Put in a large pan and add water to come level with the fruit. Bring slowly to the boil and cook for 30 minutes, until the fruit is soft and pulpy. Pour it into a jelly bag, suspend it over a bowl and leave to drip overnight. The next day measure the juice and put it in a large pan with 2 cups sugar for every 2½ cups of juice. Peel off the zest of 1 lemon and cut in thin strips; add to pan with the juice of 3 lemons. Boil up, skim until clear and simmer until setting point is reached — about 20 minutes. Skim again, pour into hot sterilized jars and cool before covering.

red currant jelly

A good jelly for eating with bread and butter, rather than meat dishes, can be made by substituting 1½ lb raspberries for half the red currants in this recipe

3 lb red currants

3 cups sugar

Take the currants off the stalks and put in a heavy pan with 1 quart water. Simmer for about 15 minutes or until mushy. Pour into a jelly bag, suspend it above a large bowl and leave to drip overnight. Next day measure the juice and put 2 cups of sugar for every 2½ cups juice into the pan. Warm the sugar in the pan, add the juice and boil for about 8 minutes, or until setting point is reached. Skim the jelly and pour into warm jars. Cover when cool and tie firmly down.

Jams, relishes and pickles

guava jelly

This is a delicacy worth making even in small quantities. It is delicious eaten with cream cheese and water biscuits

2 lb guavas

about 2 cups (1 lb) sugar

juice of 1–2 limes

Wash the guavas and cut in quarters. Put them in a pan with enough cold water to come level with the fruit. Bring to the boil, reduce heat and simmer for 30 minutes, pressing the fruit against the sides of the pan every now and then with the back of a wooden spoon, to crush it. Pour into a jelly bag, suspend it over a large bowl and leave overnight to drip. On no account try to hurry it along by stirring. Next day measure the juice and put in a heavy pan. Add 2 cups sugar and the juice of one lime for every 2½ cups of liquid. Bring to the boil and cook slowly until the sugar has dissolved, then increase the heat and boil quite hard until setting point is reached – about 20 minutes. Skim off the scum which has formed on the surface and spoon the clear liquid into hot sterilized jars. Cool and cover.

crabapple jelly

3½–4 lb crabapples

about 4 cups (2 lb) sugar

2 lemons

Pick over the fruit carefully; wash and put the whole crabapples in a heavy pan with 5 cups of water. Bring to the boil and simmer for 30 minutes. Pour into a jelly bag, suspend it over a large bowl and leave it to drip overnight. Next day, measure the juice and boil up in a pan, adding 2 cups sugar for every 2½ cups of juice. Grate the zest from the lemons and add with the lemon juice. Boil for 20–30 minutes, until setting point is reached.

Skim the jelly and pour through a sieve to remove the lemon peel. Pour into warm sterilized jars and cool before covering.

black currant jelly

2 lb black currants, or blackberries

about 4 cups (2 lb) sugar

Pick over the currants or blackberries to remove all leaves. Put in a heavy pan and add water to come level with the fruit. Bring slowly to the boil and boil for 30 minutes, crushing the currants with a wooden spoon. Pour into a jelly bag, suspend it above a large bowl and leave to drip overnight. The next day measure the juice that has dripped, pour it into a pan and add 2 cups sugar for every 2½ cups of juice. Boil together until setting point is reached. Skim and pour into warm sterilized jars. Cover when cool.

cranberry relish

Serve with hot or cold roast turkey, ham, goose, pork or duck

1 lb cranberries

1¼ cups red wine vinegar

2¼ cups firmly packed light brown sugar

2 teaspoons cinnamon

1 teaspoon salt

½ teaspoon ground cloves

1 teaspoon ground allspice

Put the cranberries in a pan with 1¼ cups water and the vinegar. Bring to the boil and simmer for 5 minutes, or until they start to burst. Press them through a medium-mesh sieve into a saucepan. Stir in the sugar, cinnamon, salt, cloves and allspice. Boil the mixture for 10–15 minutes, stirring, until it has slightly thickened. Pour into warm sterilized jars and leave to cool before sealing.

chow chow

1 *small cauliflower*
1 *lb small tomatoes*
1 *red bell pepper*
1 *green bell pepper*
6 *oz green beans*
½ *lb sweet corn kernels cut from the cob*
2½ *cups white wine vinegar*
¾ *cup light brown sugar*
1 *tablespoon mustard powder*
1 *tablespoon mustard seed*
1 *teaspoon turmeric*
8 *tablespoons coarse salt*

Cut the cauliflower into sprigs, peel the tomatoes and cut them in quarters. Cut the peppers in strips, after removing all the seeds. Trim the beans and cut in 1-inch pieces. Put all together in a large bowl with the corn kernels, and scatter the salt over them. Leave for 24 hours, then drain off the water and put the vegetables in a heavy pan. Heat the vinegar with the sugar, mustard, and turmeric and when boiling, pour over the vegetables. Bring back to the boil, cover and simmer for about 15 minutes or until they are just tender. Spoon into sterilized jars and seal. Keep for at least two weeks before opening.

mango chutney

Serve with curries of all sorts
2 *green mangoes*
3 *tablespoons coarse salt*
1¼ *cups white wine vinegar*
2 *cups light brown sugar*
2 *cloves garlic*
1 *oz fresh root ginger, chopped*
1 *teaspoon chili powder*
one 2-inch piece cinnamon stick
4 *tablespoons almonds, chopped*
⅓ *cup raisins*

Peel the mangoes and remove the seeds. Chop the flesh into small pieces and put in a bowl. Cover with the salt and pour in 4½ cups water; leave for 24 hours, then drain. Boil the vinegar with the sugar until it has dissolved. Crush the garlic and add it with the chopped ginger, chili powder and cinnamon stick. Boil for 5 minutes, then add the chopped mango and continue to boil gently for about 15 minutes or until thick. Add the chopped almonds and the raisins during the last 5 minutes. Cool and discard the cinnamon stick before spooning the mixture into sterilized jars. Keep for two weeks before eating.

chili sauce

4 *lb ripe tomatoes*
1 *lb red bell peppers*
1 *lb green bell peppers*
3 *green chili peppers*
2 *lb mild onions*
4 *cloves garlic*
1 *cup sugar*
3¾ *cups cider vinegar*
2 *tablespoons coarse salt*
1 *tablespoon ground ginger*
2 *teaspoons cinnamon*
1 *teaspoon ground cloves*
1 *teaspoon black pepper*

Peel the tomatoes and chop them roughly. Cut the red and green peppers in strips after removing the pith and seeds. Mince the chili peppers very finely after discarding all seeds. Chop the onions and mince the garlic. Put all the vegetables in a heavy pan with the vinegar, sugar and salt. Bring to the boil and simmer slowly for 2 hours, stirring occasionally. Add the spices during the last 20 minutes. Spoon into hot sterilized jars and seal. Keep for two weeks before opening.

Jams, relishes and pickles

pickled beets

In my opinion this is the best of all pickles for eating with bread and cheese

1¾ lb beets

1 medium-size onion

2 cups red wine vinegar

1½ tablespoons mustard powder

½ teaspoon coarse salt

2 cups sugar

Scrub the whole beets and cook them in plenty of water until soft. Cool slightly, reserving the cooking water, then peel and slice them. Slice the raw onion and arrange the beet and onion slices alternately in wide-mouth sterilized jars. Measure 1¼ cups of the reserved cooking water, put it in a pan and add the vinegar. Bring to the boil, then add the mustard, salt and sugar and boil again for 3 minutes. Cool slightly, then pour through a strainer into the jars to cover the beets and onion well. Close tightly. (Any extra juice can be used for pickling hard-boiled eggs, turning them pink.) Keep for at least two weeks before opening and eating.

pickled red cabbage

1 small red cabbage (about 1 lb)

1 tablespoon coarse salt

1¼ cups red wine vinegar

1 tablespoon light brown sugar

1 tablespoon pickling spice

Shred the cabbage and put it in a bowl. Sprinkle with salt and leave for 24 hours. Drain off the water, rinse the cabbage, and drain again. Pack it lightly into wide-mouthed sterilized jars. Boil the vinegar with the sugar until it has dissolved, add the pickling spice and boil for another 5 minutes. Cool, pour over the cabbage in the jars and seal tightly. Keep for two weeks before opening.

pickled onions

1 lb small white onions

¾ cup salt

2½ cups white wine vinegar

1 tablespoon light brown sugar

1 tablespoon pickling spice

Cut the tops and bottoms off the onions, but leave on the skin. Put them in a deep bowl. Bring 2 quarts of water to the boil and dissolve the salt in it, then leave to cool. Strain it, pour half over the onions. Leave for 24 hours, drain. Then peel the onions and cover with the remaining fresh brine. Weigh the onions down with a plate to keep them submerged. Leave for 48 hours. Put the vinegar in a pan with the sugar and spice and boil gently for 5 minutes; cool. Lift the onions out of the brine and pack into sterilized jars. Pour the spiced vinegar over them, let cool and seal. Keep for at least two weeks before eating.

pickled eggs

12 small eggs

4½ cups white wine vinegar

2 teaspoons black peppercorns

2 teaspoons whole allspice

2 teaspoons fresh root ginger, chopped

1 teaspoon coarse salt

Boil the eggs for 12 minutes; cool, shell and pack in large-mouth sterilized jars. Put the vinegar in a pan and add the salt and spices tied in a piece of muslin. Bring to the boil, cover the pan and simmer for 20 minutes. Turn off the heat and leave to cool for 2 hours, then remove the muslin bag. Pour the cold spiced vinegar over the eggs and seal the jars tightly. Keep for at least two weeks before opening and eating.

Desserts/sorbets

elderflower sorbet

Mint sorbet and geranium leaf sorbet can also be made with this recipe by substituting either mint sprigs or scented geranium leaves for the elderflowers

6 young elderflowers

½ cup sugar

juice of 1 lemon

1 egg white

SERVES 3

Wash the elderflowers and leave to drain. Make a thin syrup by boiling the sugar with 1¼ cups water until melted. Add the elderflowers, cover the pan and leave the mixture off the heat to infuse for 20–30 minutes. Strain into a bowl, add the lemon juice and put in an ice cream maker or freezer trays covered with foil in the freezer for 45–60 minutes. Beat the egg white, fold it into the mixture, then return the bowl to the ice cream maker or the freezer. To serve, spoon into glasses and decorate with mint or red currants and tiny wild strawberries.

strawberry and raspberry sorbet

This is delicious when accompanied with little biscuits or meringues

1 lb strawberries

¾ lb raspberries

6 tablespoons sugar

1 egg white

SERVES 4–5

Hull the berries, then put them in a blender and puree; then press through a fine sieve. Make a thin syrup by cooking the sugar with ⅝ cup water; stir into the fruit puree and taste for sweetness. Pour into an ice cream maker and freeze. Alternatively, if you do not have an ice cream maker, put the mixture in freezer trays covered with aluminum foil. After 1 hour, turn out into a bowl. Beat the egg white and fold it in. Return to the ice cream maker, or to the freezer tray, and freeze again until set.

black currant leaf sorbet

¾ cup sugar

24 young black currant leaves

juice of 1 lemon

1 egg white

SERVES 3–4

Make a syrup by boiling the sugar in 1¼ cups water, stirring until the sugar has melted. Wash the leaves, add them to the syrup, cover the pan and remove from the heat. Leave for 20 minutes. Strain, add the lemon juice and freeze in freezer trays covered with foil or an ice cream maker for 45 minutes until mushy. Spoon into a mixing bowl. Beat the egg white in another bowl and fold into the mixture. Freeze again until it is completely set.

grapefruit sorbet

2 large grapefruit

4 tablespoons sugar

1 egg white

SERVES 3–4

Squeeze and strain the juice of the grapefruit. You should have a little more than a cup. Boil the sugar in ⅝ cup water until melted, then cool. Mix this syrup with the grapefruit juice and put into freezer trays or an ice cream maker. After 45–60 minutes, when it is still mushy, beat the egg white until stiff and fold it in. Put back and freeze until ready to eat. Serve in small glasses.

peppermint ice cream

2 *eggs + 2 yolks*
4 *tablespoons sugar*
1¼ *cup milk*
1¼ *cup heavy whipping cream*
2 *tablespoons crème de menthe*
2–3 *drops green food coloring*
4 *tablespoons grated bitter chocolate*
SERVES 5–6

Beat the eggs and the yolks thoroughly. Add the sugar after a moment and continue to beat until it forms a smooth thick paste. Heat the milk until almost boiling, then pour onto the eggs, beating all the time. Set the bowl over a pan of simmering water and stir for about 8 minutes, until slightly thickened. Strain into a clean bowl and stand the bowl in a sink of cold water until cool, stirring often to prevent a skin forming. When cool, whip the cream lightly and fold it in. Stir in the crème de menthe and the green food coloring, until the mixture is a pretty pale green color. Pour into an ice cream maker and freeze until semi-frozen. Then stir in 3 tablespoons of grated chocolate and continue freezing. To serve, spoon out into a glass bowl and scatter the remaining tablespoon of grated chocolate over the top. If you do not have an ice cream maker, freeze the mixture in freezer trays, covered with aluminum foil.

black currant ice cream

1 *lb black currants*
¾ *cup sugar*
1⅞ *cup heavy whipping cream*
SERVES 6

Remove the currants from their stalks and make a syrup by boiling ⅝ cup water with ¾ cup sugar. When the sugar has melted, put in the currants. Simmer gently for 5 minutes. Press through a fine-mesh sieve and cool the mixture. Whip the cream until semi-thick and fold it in. Freeze either in an ice cream maker or, if you do not have one, in freezer trays covered with aluminum foil. In this case, stir with a fork once during freezing.

strawberry and raspberry ice cream

2 *egg yolks*
6 *tablespoons sugar*
1 *lb strawberries*
½ *lb raspberries*
juice of ½ *lemon*
⅝ *cup heavy whipping cream*
SERVES 4–6

Put the raspberries and strawberries in a blender, blend to a puree and press through a fine-mesh sieve. Beat the egg yolks with an electric beater or wire whisk while you cook the sugar with ⅝ cup water to form a thin syrup. Pour the hot syrup onto the egg yolks and continue to beat. When thick and foamy, fold in the raspberry and strawberry puree. Lightly whip the cream and fold it in with the juice of half a lemon. Pour into an ice cream maker and freeze. Alternatively, freeze the mixture in freezer trays, covered in aluminum foil, beating once with a fork during freezing. The egg whites can be made into meringues.

plum ice cream

1½ lb plums
½ cup sugar
juice of 1 orange
2 egg yolks
1¼ cups heavy whipping cream

SERVES 5–6

Cut the plums in half, remove the seeds and cut each half in several pieces. Put them in a pan with 2 tablespoons sugar, the juice of 1 orange and 2 tablespoons water. Simmer until soft, stirring often (the timing depends on the ripeness of the plums). Remove the fruit with a slotted spoon and press through a medium-mesh sieve to get rid of the skins. Boil the juice up in a pan with 6 tablespoons sugar, until reduced to about ¾ cup thin syrup. Beat the egg yolks and add the hot (nearly boiling) syrup. Continue to beat until frothy. Fold in the pureed plums. Leave to cool, then lightly whip the cream and fold it in. Freeze in an ice cream maker or, if you do not have one, freeze in freezer trays covered with aluminum foil, stirring once with a fork during freezing.

raspberry fool

This semi-frozen fool is as good as an ice cream

1 lb fresh or frozen raspberries
4 tablespoons sugar
1¼ cups heavy whipping cream

SERVES 6

Puree the raspberries in a blender, then press them through a fine-mesh sieve. Add sugar to taste. Beat the cream until it is thick but not too solid, and fold into the raspberry puree. Pour into freezer trays and place in the ice compartment of the refrigerator for 2 hours, stirring in the thickened parts at the edges of the dish once or twice. Serve in glasses and garnish with small strawberries.

orange Boodles fool

4 oranges
2 lemons
1⅞ cup heavy whipping cream
2–3 tablespoons sugar
¼ lb slightly stale sponge cake or ladyfingers

SERVES 4–5

Grate the peel from 2 oranges and 1 lemon. Squeeze the juice of all the oranges and lemons. Whip the cream lightly. Strain the fruit juices into a bowl with the half-whipped cream and add most of the grated peel. Mix. Add 2–3 tablespoons of sugar, to taste. Break the sponge cake or ladyfingers into pieces in a soufflé dish. Pour the cream mixture over the pieces, pressing them down if they float to the surface. Refrigerate for 2–3 hours. Sprinkle with the reserved grated peel before serving.

strawberry fool
with raspberry sauce

1½ lb strawberries
½ lb raspberries
½ cup sugar
⅝ cup heavy whipping cream
1–2 tablespoons light cream

SERVES 5

Put the strawberries in a blender with the sugar. Half whip the heavy cream and fold it into the puree. The result can then be pressed through a sieve if you like. Refrigerate for several hours, or put it in the freezer for an hour or so, before serving. Meanwhile make the sauce: put the raspberries in the blender, then through a fine-mesh sieve. Add sugar to taste and 1–2 tablespoons of light cream to soften the acidity. Serve the fool in a glass bowl and pass the sauce in a small pitcher.

Desserts/whips, slumps and compôtes

plum brulée

1 lb ripe plums
⅝ cup heavy whipping cream
⅝ cup sour cream
1–2 teaspoons sugar
juice of ½ lemon
2 tablespoons light brown sugar

SERVES 6

Preheat the broiler. Cut the plums in half, remove the seeds and cut in chunks. Mix the two creams together and stir in the plum pieces. Add the sugar and lemon juice. Pour into a shallow ovenproof dish. Sift an even layer of the light brown sugar over the mixture, about ⅛ inch thick. Slide under the broiler. Move it about as it browns, so that the sugar melts evenly all over. Do not let it burn. Remove as soon as it is a fairly even golden brown; cool, then chill before serving.

prune whip

¾ lb prunes
1¼ cups cold tea
2 tablespoons sugar
2 tablespoons lemon juice
⅝ cup yogurt
2 egg whites

SERVES 4

Soak the prunes overnight in the cold tea. The next day, cook them gently in the tea until soft, adding 2 tablespoons sugar. Cut out the seeds and put the prunes in a blender or food processor and puree; pour into a bowl. Beat the egg whites stiffly. Stir the lemon juice into the puree and fold in the yogurt and the egg whites. Refrigerate for two hours before serving.

apple snow

4 medium-size cooking apples
2 tablespoons sugar
2 egg whites

SERVES 4

Peel and slice the apples and put them in a saucepan with ½ cup water and the sugar. Cook until soft. Press them through a medium-mesh sieve into a bowl. Cool, then stiffly beat 2 egg whites, and fold them in. Spoon into glasses and serve with cream.

blueberry slump

A good slump can also be made with a mixture of red and white currants and cherries; the cherries should be pitted and cooked for 5 minutes longer than the currants, which only need 2–3 minutes

1 lb blueberries
4 tablespoons sugar
1¼ cups flour
1½ teaspoons baking powder
3 tablespoons butter
½ cup milk

SERVES 4–5

Wash the berries and put them to cook in a heavy pan with the sugar and just enough water to cover the bottom of the pan. Cook them gently for about 4–5 minutes until the juice starts to run. Sift the flour into a mixing bowl with the baking powder, and rub in the butter cut in small pieces, as if making pastry. Add enough milk very gradually to make a stiff dough, slightly more than you would use for pastry. (Alternatively, put flour, baking powder and butter in a food processor, and add milk while mixing.) Pat out on a board until about ½ inch thick. Cut into little rectangles roughly 1 inch square. Reheat the blueberries until simmering, lay the dough squares on top, cover the pan and cook gently for 15 minutes. Pour into a glass dish and serve hot with a small pitcher of cream.

red fruit compôte

½ lb cherries

½ lb strawberries

½ lb raspberries

½ lb red currants, or red and white currants, mixed

¾ cup sugar

SERVES 5–6

Pick the currants from their stalks and rinse all the fruit in cold water. Cut the cherries in pieces and discard the pits; halve the strawberries and hull the raspberries. Put the strawberries, raspberries and currants in a china bowl. Make a syrup by cooking the sugar in ⅝ cup water until the sugar has dissolved. Put in the cherries and simmer gently for about 4 minutes, until slightly softened. Pour the hot cherries and their syrup over the strawberries, raspberries and currants. Leave to cool. Serve warm or cool, but do not chill, and accompany with cream.

raspberry meringue

Strawberries or loganberries are also good used in this way; if frozen berries are used, allow them to thaw for only one hour before using to cover the meringue

3 egg whites

¾ cup sugar

1¼ cups heavy whipping cream

½ lb raspberries

SERVES 6

Beat the egg whites until stiff, then spoon in the sugar gradually, continuing to beat until all is absorbed. Preheat the oven to very low,

250°F. Put a piece of lightly oiled aluminum foil on a baking sheet. Spread the meringue on it in a large circle and put in the oven. Leave for about 2 hours, watching now and then to make sure the oven is not too hot. The meringue should be pale straw color by the end of the cooking time. Take the baking sheet out of the oven and leave to cool before removing the meringue from the foil. Lightly whip the cream and spread it over the meringue. Lay the raspberries over the surface of the cream and serve immediately.

peaches on meringue

2 egg whites

1¼ cups sugar

2 large ripe peaches

½ lb raspberries, fresh or frozen

2 teaspoons brandy (optional)

SERVES 4

Puree the raspberries in a blender and press through a fine-mesh nylon sieve. Stir in 2 tablespoons sugar and a little brandy if you like. Refrigerate until needed. Preheat the oven to very low, 250°F. Beat the egg whites until stiff, then add the rest of the sugar gradually, continuing to beat. When thick and smooth, spoon onto an oiled sheet of aluminum foil in four mounds. Flatten them slightly with a spatula. Bake for 1½–2 hours in the low oven, until firm and slightly colored. Cool before removing from the foil. Lay the meringue nests on a platter. Peel the peaches and place half a peach on each meringue. Pour a little of the chilled raspberry sauce over each peach before serving, and pass the rest of the sauce in a small pitcher at the table.

vacherin of red currants

3 egg whites
¾ cup sugar
1⅞ cups heavy whipping cream
½–¾ lb red currants
SERVES 6–8

Cover a flat baking sheet with a lightly oiled piece of aluminum foil. Beat the egg whites until stiff, then fold in the sugar. Preheat the oven to low, 250°F. Spoon the meringue mixture onto the foil on the baking sheet and smooth it into a round mass with a spatula. Bake for two hours, watching to see that it does not become any darker than a pale straw color. When the time is up, turn off the oven and leave the meringue inside to cool. Later, remove the meringue from the foil carefully, but do not despair if the meringue breaks. Lightly whip the cream and cover the meringue with a thick layer of whipped cream, then pile the currants on top and serve at once. A mixture of red and white currants can be used, but the color should be mainly red to contrast with the meringue and cream.

raspberry and red currant tart

¾ lb raspberries
½ lb red currants
⅜ cup sugar
2 cups sifted flour
½ cup (1 stick) butter
4 tablespoons (2 oz) lard
2 egg yolks
1 teaspoon lemon juice
SERVES 6

Pick over the fruit, wash it well and put it in a bowl. Make the pastry as follows. Rub the butter and lard into the flour and add ½ teaspoon sugar. Stir in 1 egg yolk and the lemon juice, then about 3 tablespoons of ice water to make a firm dough. Handling the dough as little as possible, enclose in plastic wrap and refrigerate for 30 minutes. Roll out the dough on a floured surface and use it to line a large flan tin or ovenproof dish. Chill again for 30 minutes and preheat the oven to 400°F. Beat the remaining egg yolk, brush it over the pastry and prick the pastry here and there with a fork. Bake for 10 minutes, turn the heat down to 350°F and bake for a further 10 minutes. Pile the raspberries and currants mixed with sugar into the shell and return to the oven for 5 minutes. Serve immediately.

blueberry pancakes

2 cups flour
¼ teaspoon salt
½ teaspoon sugar
2 eggs
1¼ cups milk
¾–1 cup blueberries
SERVES 6

If making the batter by hand, sift the flour into a bowl and make a depression in the center. Break in the eggs. Put the milk and 1¼ cups water in a pitcher. Start to beat the eggs with a wire whisk while gradually incorporating the flour from around the edges, at the same time pouring in the milk and water mixture, in a thin stream. When all the flour is amalgamated, the liquid should also be absorbed. Add the salt and sugar, and continue to beat for a minute or two. Stand for an hour before using. Alternatively, the batter can be quickly made in a food processor. Just before using the batter, fold in the berries, but first heat the griddle or frying pan until very hot indeed. Pour on a big spoonful of the batter, with some blueberries in it, and cook for about 3 minutes, turning once.

Austrian plum dumplings

2¼ cups self-rising flour
½ teaspoon salt
⅝ cup milk
¾ cup (1½ stick) butter
1 egg + 1 yolk
10–12 small or 5–6 large ripe plums
3 tablespoons dry bread crumbs
2 tablespoons poppy seeds

SERVES 5–6

Sift the flour and salt into a large bowl. Heat the milk with 4 tablespoons (½ stick) of the butter until it reaches boiling point. Pour immediately into the bowl with the flour, and mix well with a wooden spoon. Beat together the egg and the extra yolk and stir in. Mix until smooth and well blended. Roll out on a floured surface and cut into small circles about ¼ inch thick. Remove the plum seeds. Put one small plum, or a half of a large one, in the center of each circle of dough and bring up the dough carefully around it, sealing the edges. Put into boiling water and poach for about 8 minutes. Drain carefully. Melt 1 tablespoon butter and fry the dry bread crumbs in it until they turn golden brown. Mix in the poppy seeds. Roll each dumpling in this mixture. Melt the rest of the butter and serve it with the dumplings in a small pitcher.

plum tart

¾ lb short pastry (see recipe, page 126)
1 egg yolk
1 lb dark red plums
2 tablespoons sugar
4 tablespoons raspberry, crabapple, or red currant jelly

Make the short pastry and chill for about 30 minutes, then roll out on a floured surface and line a large dish or tin. Preheat the oven to 400°F. Beat the egg yolk and brush over the pastry. Bake for 10 minutes, remove from the oven and cool slightly. Reduce heat to 350°F. Wash and cut up the plums thickly, removing the seeds and retaining the juices. Put the plum pieces with their juices into the pastry shell. Sprinkle with the sugar and bake for 25 minutes. Put the jelly in a small pan and heat gently. When the tart is cooked, remove it from the oven and pour off the juice into a pan, or extract it with a baster; boil up to reduce it, in order to intensify the flavor, if you wish, and mix about 2 tablespoons of it with the jelly, to make a glaze. The proportions should never be more juice than half the jelly amount, or it will not thicken enough to use as a glaze. Stir until blended, then spoon or brush over the surface of the plums. This tart is best if eaten within an hour of baking, but is also good cool; it should not be chilled. If it is to be eaten cool, brush again with the glaze once or twice while it cools.

plums in yogurt

1 lb ripe plums
⅝ cup heavy whipping cream
⅝ cup yogurt
1 egg white
2 tablespoons sugar

SERVES 4

Cut the plums in half, remove the seeds and cut each half in several pieces, retaining the juices. Divide among four glass bowls. Beat the cream until fairly stiff and fold in the yogurt. Then stiffly beat the egg white, add the sugar and fold it in. Spoon the mixture generously over the plums and refrigerate until ready to serve.

caramel meringue

4 eggs

7 tablespoons vanilla sugar (see recipe, page 126), or 7 tablespoons sugar and ½ vanilla pod

2 cups milk

½ cup sugar

SERVES 5–6

First make the caramel: put the ½ cup plain sugar in a heavy pan with ½ cup water and bring slowly to the boil. Continue to boil slowly and steadily until it starts to caramelize and turn a pale golden color. Take immediately from the heat, as the color turns very rapidly and it will burn within a matter of seconds. Pour it into a tin cake mold or an ovenproof dish and turn it quickly so that the inside is coated more or less all over with the golden caramel. Leave to harden while you make the meringue. Preheat oven to 325°F. Separate the eggs and beat the whites until stiff. Fold in 4 tablespoons vanilla sugar, or plain sugar if you haven't made vanilla sugar. Pile the meringue into the caramel-lined mold and put in a baking tin half-filled with water. Stand it in the oven and bake for 20 minutes. Meanwhile make the custard: beat the egg yolks for several minutes with an electric beater until thick and creamy. Heat the milk with the remaining 3 tablespoons vanilla sugar until almost boiling, then pour into the egg yolks, continuing to beat. (If you have no vanilla sugar, heat the milk with the piece of vanilla pod in it, and leave, covered, for 10 minutes; then remove the pod, reheat the milk until almost boiling and pour into the egg yolks.) Stand the bowl in a saucepan of simmering water and stir until slightly thickened. Then remove and set to cool in a sink of cold water. When the meringue and sauce are cool, refrigerate for 2 hours. Turn out the meringue and pour the sauce around.

caramel mousse

¾ cup sugar

1¼ cups heavy whipping cream

2 envelopes (½ oz) powdered gelatine

4 egg whites

SERVES 4

Put the sugar in a heavy pan with ¾ cup water. Heat gently until a pale golden, then remove from the heat. Pour one-third of this caramel into an oiled pan and refrigerate. Whip the cream until thick. When the rest of the caramel is just cool enough to allow you to dip your finger in it without pain, pour it onto the cream and stir it in. (If it forms into a hard toffee, lift out the solid parts with a slotted spoon and put back in the pan with some of the cream; stir over gentle heat until melted and blended with the cream, then pour back into the rest of the cream and mix well.) Soften the gelatine in 2 tablespoons of cold water in a heatproof cup, then place cup in a shallow pan of simmering water to melt gelatine. When dissolved, stir into the caramel cream. Beat the egg whites until stiff, then fold in. Pour into a soufflé dish and refrigerate until set. When ready to serve, take the thin layer of hard caramel from the refrigerator and break it by hitting it with the back of a spoon. Scatter the fragments of caramel over the top of the mousse and serve.

oeufs en neige (floating island)

3 eggs

4 tablespoons vanilla sugar (see recipe, page 126)

1⅞ cups milk

SERVES 4–5

Separate the yolks from the whites. Beat 2 of the whites until stiff, and fold in half the vanilla sugar to make a meringue mixture. Put plenty of water in a large pan and heat it to simmering point. Drop in the meringue mixture in tablespoons, and poach gently, only a few at a time, so that they do not touch each other. After about 3 minutes, turn them over with a slotted spoon and poach for a further 2–3 minutes. Lift them out and drain on a cloth (they will stick to paper) while you poach the rest. When well drained, lift them off the cloth onto a flat plate and refrigerate. Beat the egg yolks with the remaining vanilla sugar. Heat the milk almost to boiling point and pour into the bowl with the egg yolk and sugar mixture. Set the bowl over a pan of boiling water and stir until slightly thickened; then set in cold water to cool, stirring occasionally. Refrigerate for a few hours. To serve, pour the custard sauce into a shallow bowl and lay the meringues on it.

caramel junket

4 *tablespoons sugar*
2½ *cups milk*
1 *rennet tablet (available from pharmacists or health food shops)*
2 *tablespoons heavy whipping cream*

SERVES 4–5

Put the sugar in a heavy pan with about 2 tablespoons water and heat it gently until it reaches a pale golden color. Meanwhile, bring ⅝ cup milk almost to boiling point; add to pan gradually, stirring hard to blend the two. If they refuse to mix and the caramel forms into toffee, simply drain off the milk, reheat the toffee until soft, and pour in the milk again. When amalgamated, pour into a bowl and leave to cool until lukewarm. Gently heat the rest of the milk until tepid, and stir in the caramel. Cool to 98°F. Dissolve the rennet tablet in 1 tablespoon water and stir into the mixture. Whip the cream and spoon over.

junket

2½ *cups milk*
½ *tablespoon sugar*
1 *rennet tablet (available from pharmacists or health food shops)*
pinch of grated nutmeg or cinnamon

SERVES 3–4

This old-fashioned English dish should be made with milk still warm from the cow. Failing this, the milk should be gently heated until it reaches body temperature, about 98°F. Stir in the sugar. Crush the rennet tablet and dissolve in 1 tablespoon cold water; add to the mixture and pour into a dish. Leave at room temperature to set. Before serving, sprinkle with nutmeg or cinnamon.

peaches in gelatine

4 *large peaches*
¾ *cup sugar*
juice of 2 lemons
1 *envelope (¼ oz) powdered gelatine*

SERVES 6

Peel the peaches, cut them in half and remove the seeds. Put the sugar in a pan with ¾ cup water and heat, stirring, to make a thin syrup. Put in enough of the halved peaches to fit comfortably in one layer and poach for a few minutes, turning once. Lift them out carefully and drain, while you poach the rest. When all are done, squeeze the juice of the lemons into the syrup and measure it. With any luck you should have about 1¼ cups; if not, make it up to this measure with water or fruit juice. Dissolve the gelatine in about 2 tablespoons of water and stir into the syrup. Lay the peaches in a round flat dish and pour the liquid over them through a strainer. Only half-cover them, so that the peaches rise above the gelatine. Refrigerate until set.

orange gelatine

5–6 *oranges*
1 *lemon*
½ *cup* + 1 *tablespoon sugar*
2 *envelopes (½ oz) powdered gelatine*

SERVES 4

Grate the peel of 2 of the oranges and half the lemon. Put in a bowl and squeeze the juice of all the oranges and the lemon over it. Put the sugar in a small pan with 1¼ cups water; bring to the boil and simmer until the sugar has melted and the liquid has slightly reduced. Pour the fruit juice with the grated peel into the pan and bring back to the boil. Skim off any scum that rises to the surface; add a tablespoon of cold water and skim again. Half-fill a pan with water and bring to the boil, then take from the heat. Soften the gelatine in a bowl in 2 tablespoons of cold water and stir, standing the bowl in a pan half-full of hot water until the gelatine is melted. Add to the fruit juice, stir well, then pour the mixture through a strainer into a measuring pitcher. You should have 2½ cups. If you have less, add some more orange juice or water. Pour into a ring mold and cool, then refrigerate until set. Turn out on a flat dish.

lemon gelatine

4 *large lemons*
¾ *cup sugar*
1½ *envelopes (⅜ oz) powdered gelatine*

SERVES 4

Cut the zest off the lemons, slice it thinly and put it in a bowl. Squeeze the juice from the lemons. Put the sugar in 1¼ cups boiling water, cook until it has melted, then pour it while still boiling over the lemon zest. Cover and stand for 20 minutes. Strain into a bowl. Dissolve the gelatine in a little of the strained syrup and add with the lemon juice to the mixture in the bowl. Measure it and make it up to 2½ cups by adding water if necessary. Strain again into a ring mold and chill until set. Turn it out on a flat dish and serve with cream, whipped cream or yogurt.

apples with toffee sauce

6 *cooking apples*
3–4 *plums*
3 *slices dry bread*
½ *cup* + 1 *tablespoon light brown sugar*
4 *tablespoons (½ stick) butter, at room temperature*
2 *tablespoons heavy whipping cream*

SERVES 6

Core, but do not peel the apples. Chop the plums after removing the seeds. Cut the bread in six rounds. Butter a baking pan and lay the bread rounds in it; put one apple on each one. Fill the centers of the apples with chopped plums. Preheat the oven to 400°F. Mix the brown sugar and the butter to a paste; dot around the baking pan. Bake for 30 minutes, basting the apples now and then with the pan juices. Lift them carefully on their pieces of bread and transfer to a serving dish. Put the baking pan over a gentle heat and stir the cream into the toffee mixture that the pan juices will have formed. Pour this sauce into a pitcher and serve with the apples. If no plums are available, the apples can be filled simply with the butter and sugar mixture; the bread will soak up the juices during the cooking. Or the bread can be fried separately and put under the plum-filled apples at the last minute.

chocolate apple cream

I always thought this dish, much loved by children of our family, was special to us as I had never seen it anywhere else. Recently, however, I came across what must have been the original recipe, in a book called *Caviare to Candy*, by Mrs Philip Martineau, published in 1923 and long out of print

2 *lb cooking apples*

4 *tablespoons sugar*

1¼ *cups heavy whipping cream*

two 1 *oz squares good bittersweet chocolate*

SERVES 4

Peel and slice the apples, and cook them with the sugar in a pan with a little water. Press through a medium-mesh sieve. When cool, spoon the mixture into a flat layer in the bottom of a serving dish. Whip the cream until thick but not solid and spoon over the apple mixture. Grate the chocolate and sprinkle over the cream. Chill for 2–3 hours before serving.

tuiles

To make this dish into the classic French *tuiles d'amandes*, add 2 tablespoons coarsely chopped almonds to the mixture before baking in the oven

4 *tablespoons (½ stick) butter*

4 *tablespoons sugar*

4 *tablespoons flour*

MAKES ABOUT 12 TUILES

Preheat the oven to 350°F. Cream the butter and the sugar together and stir in the flour. Make 12 small round balls with a teaspoon and put them on a lightly greased baking sheet, well spaced out and only five at a time. Bake for 6–8 minutes, until evenly spread out and pale golden with slightly darker edges. Take them out of the oven and wait for half a minute before attempting to lift them off the baking sheet with a spatula. As soon as they can be moved without breaking, lay them over an oiled wine bottle to cool. If they cool and become stiff while still on the baking sheet, replace it for a moment in the oven to soften them again. When cool and firm, slide carefully off the bottle and lay on a flat dish.

strawberry shortcake

½ *lb strawberries*

2 *cups sifted flour*

2 *teaspoons double-acting baking powder*

½ *teaspoon salt*

3 *tablespoons sugar*

4 *tablespoons (½ stick) butter*

¾ *cup milk and cream, mixed*

1¼ *cups heavy whipping cream*

SERVES 6

Sift the flour with the baking powder, salt and 1 tablespoon sugar. Cut in, then rub in, the butter; alternatively use a food processor. Add the milk and cream, and stir until the mixture forms a soft dough. Preheat the oven to 450°F. Knead lightly a couple of times on a floured board, then divide into two unequal pieces. Roll or pat out into two rounds about ½ inch thick, one slightly larger than the other. Lay on two oiled baking sheets and bake for 12–15 minutes, until a pale golden brown. Cool on a rack for about 15 minutes. Lightly whip the cream. Cut two-thirds of the strawberries in half, reserving a third of them whole, for garnish, and mix with the sugar. Spread the larger circle of pastry with the lightly whipped cream and the sugared strawberries. Place the smaller pastry round on top, press lightly and decorate with the reserved whole strawberries and the rest of the whipped cream; serve at once.

cheese scones

1 cup sifted flour
2 teaspoons baking powder
½ teaspoon salt
1 teaspoon mustard powder
⅝ cup freshly grated Cheddar cheese
4 tablespoons (½ stick) butter or margarine
1 medium-size egg
⅝ cup milk
2 tablespoons grated Parmesan cheese

MAKES 12 SCONES

Sift the flour with the baking powder and salt. Add the mustard powder, grated Cheddar and the butter or margarine, cut in small pieces. Rub in quickly, or mix in a mixer. Beat the egg with the milk and add enough of it to the flour mixture to form a soft dough. Enclose in plastic wrap and refrigerate for half an hour. Preheat the oven to 400°F. Roll out the dough on a floured surface to about ½ inch thick and cut into shapes with an oval or round cutter. Place on a buttered baking sheet, sprinkle with grated Parmesan, and bake near the top of the oven for 8–10 minutes, or until puffed up and golden brown. Test one to make sure it is cooked through; if not, put lower down in the oven for 3 minutes. Serve with butter.

cinnamon toast

4 slices white bread
2 tablespoons butter
2 tablespoons sugar
½ teaspoon powdered cinnamon

SERVES 4

Toast the bread lightly and remove the crusts. Mix the sugar and cinnamon together in a cup. Spread butter on each slice of bread and sprinkle on the sugar and cinnamon mixture. Place under the broiler until the sugar has melted and turned a golden brown.

brownies

four 1oz squares unsweetened chocolate
½ cup (1 stick) butter
4 eggs
1¼ cups sugar
1 cup flour
¼ lb shelled walnuts (optional)
pinch of salt

MAKES 16 BROWNIES

Break the chocolate in small pieces and put with the butter in a bowl over a pan of boiling water. Preheat the oven to 350°F. As the butter and chocolate melt, mix them well. Remove the bowl from the pan and cool. Beat the eggs thoroughly and stir in the salt and sugar. Stir in the cooled chocolate mixture, then the sifted flour and chopped nuts, if including. Mix lightly and quickly. Pour into a shallow, well-greased baking pan about 10 inches square. Bake for 35 minutes or until lightly colored. Brownies should be slightly soft in the middle, so be careful not to overcook them. Take from the heat and cool. Cut into squares and serve with a bowl of whipped cream.

oatjacks

6 tablespoons (¾ stick) butter
¾ cup light brown sugar
½ cup breakfast oats

MAKES 9 SMALL CAKES

Put the butter in a pan and heat gently. As soon as it has melted, stir in the sugar and remove from the heat. Preheat the oven to 350°F. Mix the oats into the butter and sugar mixture and turn into a well-buttered, shallow 8-inch square baking pan. Bake for about 15 minutes or until golden brown all over. Leave to cool before cutting.

Drinks

carrot and tomato juice

1 lb carrots
1 lb tomatoes
⅝ cup yogurt (optional)
2 tablespoons lemon juice
1 tablespoon orange juice

SERVES 3–4

Put the carrots and then the tomatoes in a juice extractor. Mix the two juices together and stir in the yogurt, if you want a more substantial mixture. Stir in the lemon and orange juices, mix and chill before serving.

sorrel and buttermilk drink

½ lb sorrel
1¼ cups buttermilk
1¼ cups yogurt

SERVES 4

Put the sorrel in a juice extractor. Put the juice in a blender or food processor. Add the buttermilk and yogurt and blend, then chill before serving.

mango and orange drink

This is nutritious as well as refreshing, since mangoes are rich in vitamin C

1 ripe mango
2 tablespoons sugar
1¼ cups orange juice
6 tablespoons lime juice

SERVES 3–4

Peel the mango, cut up the flesh and put into a blender or food processor, scraping all the juicy parts from the seed as well. Heat 1¼ cups water, add the sugar and stir until the sugar has melted to form a thin syrup; cool. Blend the chopped mango with the sugar syrup and the fruit juices. Chill, and serve in glasses over ice cubes.

buttermilk and watercress drink

2½ cups buttermilk
⅝ cup yogurt
1 bunch watercress

SERVES 4

Put the buttermilk and yogurt in a blender or food processor with the leaves of the watercress. Blend, pour into glasses and chill.

cucumber and yogurt drink

1 cucumber
2½ cups yogurt
1 tablespoon chopped mint
pinch of salt

SERVES 4

Peel the cucumber and cut it in chunks. Put in a blender with the yogurt and salt, and three cracked ice cubes. Blend, stir in the fresh mint and blend again. Chill before pouring into glasses and serving.

currant cordial

½ lb white currants
2½ cups brandy
pinch of ground ginger
zest of ½ lemon
sugar as required

Pick the currants from their stalks and crush them in a china bowl. Pour the brandy over them. Cut the zest from the lemon in fine strips and add to the bowl with the ginger. Stir well and cover the bowl with foil. Let stand for 24 hours at room temperature, stirring now and then. Strain through damp muslin or doubled cheesecloth and measure. Add ¾ cup sugar for every 2½ cups of liquid. Stir until the sugar has dissolved, then bottle.

Basic recipes

basic white sauce

1¼ cups milk, or stock of chicken, fish or vegetables
1 thin slice onion
2 cloves
¼ bay leaf
3 tablespoons butter
2 tablespoons flour
pinch of grated nutmeg
salt and pepper

If using milk and no other flavoring is to be added to the white sauce, the milk should be infused before adding: put it into a small pan with the onion, cloves, and bay leaf. Bring slowly to the boil and immediately remove from the heat. Cover the pan and let stand for 20 minutes. Melt the butter slowly in a heavy pan. Remove from the heat and shake in the flour, stirring until amalgamated. Return to the heat and cook for 1–2 minutes, stirring constantly. Remove from the heat again. Strain the heated milk. Pour it (or the stock) gradually into the pan, stirring constantly until blended. Return to the heat and bring to the boil, stirring. Simmer gently for at least 4 minutes, stirring now and then. Add salt and pepper to taste and the grated nutmeg. Grated cheese or cream should be added at this stage; chopped herbs should be added only at the last moment. This sauce can be served immediately or kept warm over a pan of hot water until needed; in this case beat well before serving.

vanilla sugar

3–4 vanilla pods
2¼ cups sugar

Put the sugar into a glass jar and stick a few vanilla pods upright into the sugar. Fill up the jar with the rest of the sugar and close tightly. Leave for at least a week before using, to allow the vanilla flavor to permeate the sugar. Some people cut the pods in half lengthwise, which increases the flavor, but this gives a sticky brown substance to the sugar, which I find unattractive. If required for another use, a pod can be taken out of the sugar, and used to flavor a dish, then carefully washed, well dried, and replaced in the jar. I find this is rarely necessary, however, as I do not often seem to need the flavor of vanilla without the sweetness of the sugar. As it is used up, the sugar can be replenished; the pods will only need replacing after a year or so.

basic short pastry

When a recipe calls for ½lb pastry, use the quantities given here. When a recipe calls for 6oz pastry, make this quantity and put aside a quarter of it. Where a recipe calls for ¾lb pastry, make double the quantity, and put aside a quarter, for another use. For a sweet dish, omit the salt and add a pinch of sugar and a squeeze of lemon juice

2 cups sifted flour
pinch of salt
½ cup (1 stick) butter
¼ cup lard

Make sure both the butter and lard are very cold indeed before starting, and have some ice water available. Sift the flour with the salt into a large bowl. Cut the butter and lard in small pieces and rub them into the flour very quickly; then add just enough ice water to make a soft dough, mixing with the blade of a knife. Handling it as little as possible, form it in a ball, enclose in plastic wrap, and refrigerate for 30 minutes before using.

Index

Page numbers in italics refer to illustrations. Page numbers in bold refer to recipes, and all other numbers refer to text.